Living Landscapes

Waterways

First published in Great Britain in 2004
The National Trust Enterprises Ltd
36 Queen Anne's Gate
London
SW1H 9AS
www.nationaltrust.org.uk

ISBN 0 7078 0347 0

www.james-crowden.co.uk

Cataloguing in Publication Data is available from the British Library

Designed and art directed by Wildlife Art Ltd/www.wildlife-art.co.uk

All colour artwork by Bryn Edwards/Wildlife Art Ltd

Cover by Yellow Box Design with original artwork by Alison Lang

Printed and bound in Italy by G. Canale & C.s.p.A

Living Landscapes

Waterways

James Crowden

🌿 THE NATIONAL TRUST

Contents

FACING PAGE: Beginner's Way. Jamie McCullough's wooden stepping stones in a forest outside Exeter in Devon. Jamie spent two years living alone in the forest and made this one-and-a-half-mile trail with 22 wooden sculptures and works of art. Over half a million visitors walked and experienced the trail in its seven-year life.

Acknowledgements

Waterways are strange beasts. Once you are hooked there is no getting away from them. You peer into every ditch and stream just to check which way it is flowing. You demand to know which river or canal it is that you have just crossed at high speed. You want to understand where your water is going and where it has come from. Researching waterways has therefore been fascinating and my only regret is that I could not spend several more years pottering in backwaters asking obscure questions or simply observing the way the light falls on a river, or a swan's back, or a canal.

My thanks are due to the many people up and down the country who have answered questions or put me up for the night. Thanks to Fiona Screen and James Parry of the National Trust as editors, to wildlife artist Bryn Edwards and to Warrender Grant for the design. Thanks also to Lewis Eynon from Cotehele, Keith Sherwin at Arkwright's Mill in Cromford, Michael Brown for information on elvers, smoked eels and eel migrations, Gyles Morris of Magdalen Farm Dorset, Nick and Ruth Pitts Tucker, Peter Irvine, Roger Deakin, Christopher Culpin, Guy Crowden, Sue Clifford and Angela King of Common Ground, Carol Trewin, David Prysor Jones, Peter Milner, Tom Greeves, Serena de la Hey, Evelyn Body, Fiona Mason, Chris Lawson of the Environment Agency Exeter, Martin Williams of the Environment Agency Cornwall, Darryl Clifton-Dey of the Environment Agency Reading, Simon Coton of Welsh Water, Giles White, Johnne Abrams, Katrina Porteous, Roy Fisher, Craig Raine, Stephen Capel Davies of Wisbech Museum, Caroline Elkerton, Richard Venters, Richard Macrory, Bill Blackburne, Eliot Morley, David Laws, John Goodridge, Kelsey Thornton, Paul Dawson, The Royal Geographical Society Map Room, and many others whose goodwill and information was invaluable. Water and waterways will never be the same again.

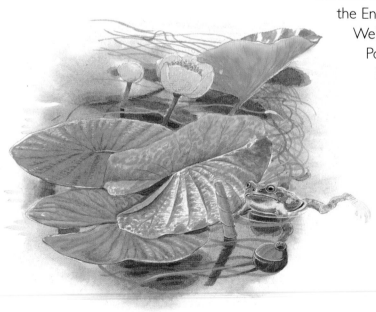

Foreword

Water inspires all of us. Somehow it always imparts some of its own agility, grace and clarity to whoever wanders or settles beside it. So what good sense to invite a poet, James Crowden, to write this book. All poets feel a natural affinity with running water, with its dancing rhythms and cadences, its sudden changes of mood and tempo, its unique power to refresh and to heal. Anyone who has witnessed a great river in flood will also understand its sheer elemental force. No wonder our ancestors revered the springs and rivers as sacred. Rivers and streams have carved out and fashioned the very land itself, first as ice then as restless, wandering eels, forever shifting course across country down the ages.

The playfulness of water is infectious. It brings out the otter or the engineer in all of us, especially as children, when we love to splash about in the least puddle, or dam a burn to make a waterfall. The enduring popularity of Ratty and Mole in *The Wind in the Willows*, Henry Williamson's great *Tarka the Otter* or Charles Kingsley's *The Water Babies* suggests a deep feeling of kinship with riverbank life in the national psyche. Canals, too, inspire the same lively impulse to give rein to the imagination. They stand for the vision, ingenuity and plain hard work of the original bold navigators. And they still offer one of the best alternatives I know to life in the fast lane: that of the water gypsy.

In *The Age of Scandal*, his splendid book about eighteenth-century gossip and the letter-writer Horace Walpole, T.H. White tells the story of a sumptuous dinner given by the Duke of Queensberry at his villa by the Thames. William Pitt was there, and so was the young William Wilberforce, who wrote later of the villa's enchanting views of the river in all its glory, but of how the Duke looked on with indifference. 'What is there,' he said, 'to make so much of in the Thames? – I am quite tired of it – there it goes, flow, flow, flow, always the same.'

Fortunately, James Crowden takes an altogether different view of our rivers and waterways: erudite, poetic, romantic, and full of fascinating detail. I warmly commend it to you.

Roger Deakin
Writer and broadcaster, author of *Waterlog*

Introduction

Waterways – and the wily ways of water – are an integral part of our living, working landscape. They shape, form and define the countryside around us, and are a potent cultural symbol that speaks to us on a variety of different levels, from the prosaic to the deeply spiritual. We all carry the image of water in our imagination, and are all connected to it in some way. Most of us live near a river in some shape or form, even if it has been consigned to a subterranean, culverted existence far away from our gaze and contemplation. Yet we barely understand what an important part of our lives water really plays, or how water, in its many guises, has shaped our landscape, both naturally and at our specific and contrived behest.

Rivers flow…wells spring, fountains beckon; streams, brooks, lodes and winterbournes twist and turn. Burns, rills, rillets and rivulets run helter-skelter down gills and gullies, vales and dales. Leats, launders, canals and lock gates; rhines, clyses, weirs and sluices; ditches, drains, dams, lakes and reservoirs. All of these features channel, control or contain water. They are a source of movement, influence and confluence – of power and dispute. So much more than just blue lines on the map. Waterways serve as political boundaries, social demarcators, cultural indicators, economic opportunities, valuable wildlife habitat. They are living history.

This book is concerned with all these things, from chalk streams to archbishops' palaces, from water bailiffs to crayfish, moats to water privatisation. It is the story not just of British waterways and the features and practices associated with them, but of our common history, for almost anything of any import has happened in, on, or along our streams, rivers and canals. From the Somerset Levels to the Manchester Ship Canal, the Norfolk Broads to the River Tweed, waterways bear witness to every significant event in British history. They are the lodestone that has directed the course of our development.

As a poet, I make no apology for the approach I bring to this subject. The evolution of waterways fascinates me: the metamorphosis from inauspicious hillside trickle to mighty turbine of town and industry. Yet this is as much a book of artistic celebration, of the inspiration that countless generations have derived from the watery landscapes of Britain, as an historical account. Waterways demand sacrifice and poetry. They want to be photographed and painted, admired and described. Why should they conform to the straitjacket of facts and events? They are worth more than this. Water is a mirror, and in it we see ourselves. Water is life itself.

My poem, *In Time of Flood*, graphically documents the way in which the River Parrett rises, bursts its banks and then floods large areas of the Somerset Levels and Moors. The wonderful flowing calligraphy is by Jenni Harrison.

In Time of Flood – The River Parrett
JAMES CROWDEN

Rain and river run, wild waters rise, REBELLIOUS
SUCCULENT and SINUOUS, each sensuous bend
Winding its way seaward, curved currents brim
Heady in hidden depths, brown banks burst their bodice,
Merge and overspill, breathe more freely, let go in reams,
The heavy water's cargo, swift in silt,
Slowly seeping, draws the land down, sodden and submerged,
Steeped and stored, sprawled and spread, the temper eased,
Wanders dark and quivering between the withy beds
Rhines held hostage, a silent shallow haunting,
Without a ripple the flood's quiet carpet runs for miles
A strange mirror held up to the eye
Polished and poised, the slice of light,
The watter's sheen-shimmer skimming rank sedge
Reed-rustled and ruckled, the reflected light-dazzle
Strewn and scattered, the sudden furious flurry of small waves
Weaving and weary-worn, the slither of silver meadows
A shining shawl of pearls, a shoal of fresh fish
Flung glittering in the gloaming, a glad glimmer
A gauntlet thrown down, THE RIVER'S VOICE,
THE RAIN'S TORRID MAJESTY, TURBULENT and TEMPESTUOUS
The hidden pulse pushing at walls and bridges,
Sluices and weirs, in full pelt, nudging towns and trees
The flood's free measure, rampant and flowing,
Fuelled by further distant downpours. Each gate
A window through which the light slides, an inland sea
Where the river meets the sky, the scudding source
Sharp and clear, stark and gaunt, sunken, the winter ground
Pollarded and punctuated, stumps of withy, sore thumbs
Hoisted on the horizon, silhouetted and silent
Like witnesses after an execution, the land drowned,
The sky stretched and stretching, taught like a canvas,
A staunch saddle over which geese wheel.

Chapter One

❖

Water at source

PREVIOUS SPREAD The Victorian fountain and fernery at Greenway in Devon.

WATER AT SOURCE

Ariadne, 'Nymph of the Grot', based on a classical figure in the Vatican Gardens and found at the source of the River Stour at Stourhead in Wiltshire. Crystal-clear spring water is channelled from the chalk aquifer to emerge from beneath the reclining Ariadne.

For many people the sight of water bubbling up from an underground source is irresistible. There is an air of mystery and intrigue, a sense of theatre, as if we are party to a natural miracle. It is more than just the fluidity of the water coming to the surface; something symbolic and unspoken, almost personal, is involved, as if the spring has a deep-seated meaning beyond our normal everyday language. It is precisely this sense of mystery into which many religions have tapped. Throughout history, springs and wells have become places of divination, shrines to healing, expressions of thanks and somewhere to quench one's thirst – natural phenomena to be celebrated and revered.

The spring

As well as epitomising birth and divine providence, springs also symbolise the beginning of long journeys, of the inexorable progression of stream into river into sea, in an evolution of various forms. The very word 'spring' has many meanings – it can signify movement, a time of year when the forces of life are at their most vibrant and dynamic, a dance, a lively tune, all of which were surely not lost on the composer Stravinsky when he wrote his incredibly powerful and pagan offering, *The Rite of Spring*.

One of the strangest rituals connected with springs and water sources is that of divining – our ability to sense water when we cannot see it. To feel the hazel rods twitching in your fingertips is a bizarre experience, an intriguing connection between the seen and unseen. Even the word divine has within it the germ of devotion, a form of spiritual quest. And as the diviner seeks out water, so poets seek out new paths in our speech, trying to convey thoughts and emotions and mapping the deep patterns of our psychological aquifer. Words and streams are similar: we talk of people babbling on, a flood of ideas, a speech causing ripples or someone's thoughts having dried up. Seamus Heaney has often alluded to the poet's task as being akin to that of the water diviner:

Unfussed. The pluck came sharp as a sting.
The rod jerked with precise convulsions
Spring water suddenly broadcasting
Through a green hazel its secret stations

from *The Diviner* by Seamus Heaney

An illustration from Agricola's *De Re Metallica* (1557), showing two diviners at work with hazel rods, looking for water and minerals. Minerals such as tin are often found in old underground streams where water has washed the deposits from a lode.

Water divining or dowsing is an ancient skill. The earliest record of it is at least 5,000 years old and appears on a grave inscription in Brittany. In practical terms, water divining is the act of searching for underground water with the use of a forked hazel rod. The diviner slowly walks across the land holding the rod, one branch in each hand, and when he or she passes over a possible source of water the rod dips significantly. The hazel rod is not obligatory; welding rods or even coat hangers have produced results. Various theories have been put forward over the years to explain this involuntary movement of the rod, but the most likely explanation is that it has something to do with small magnetic or electrical fields, which may relate to changes in geology. To this day the skill is not fully understood by conventional science and is regarded as a subconscious art relying more on minute observation and instinct than on psychic powers. Nevertheless, some water diviners are able to make a living from their skill, for example they are employed by farmers to advise them on where to sink boreholes.

Not surprisingly, divining ran into trouble with the Church. Even the great Protestant reformer Martin Luther stated (in 1518) that the use of the divining rod broke the first commandment. No doubt he preferred divine intervention of another kind.

The very natural phenomenon of water gushing or issuing from the ground has always inspired belief, incredulity and gratitude, spawning in turn a whole host of myths and legends, ceremonies and rituals. In these days of hot and cold mixer taps, central heating, jacuzzis, lawn sprinklers and automatic car washes, we have no real notion of the origins of water, or even of the ways in which it has formed and shaped our society. Yet since the beginning of human existence the location and maintenance of clean and reliable water sources has been one of mankind's foremost concerns. Hunter-gatherers would track animals to and from waterholes, following seasonal migrations and attempting to

This extraordinarily accurate illustration from *De Re Metallica* (1557) shows not only a hand pump working down a mine, and all the ancillary parts, but also the act of boring pipes from tree trunks. In Britain wooden pipes were used well into the nineteenth century, the best wood being elm, as it was strong, had uneven grain and was resistant to water.

read the landscape in terms of the availability of water. Those among them who were skilled in the detection of water were no doubt revered and listened to. As man gradually settled into a less peripatetic life and established an agricultural routine, his need for water was no less great. Indeed, in some respects it grew, with the increased demand for water to grow crops and sustain domestic livestock.

The most obvious solution to the water issue was to settle near a readily accessible source, such as a spring, river or lake. Good-quality, reliable springs were always at a premium, and their presence was often the catalyst for a settlement to develop nearby. Hamlets and villages literally sprang up.

The well

In locations where springs did not naturally occur, it was necessary to dig down to reach the aquifers underground and then draw the water up to the surface by hand or by beast. In other words, wells were created. Historically, wells were dug by hand, to a depth below the water table, when the amount of water filling the excavated hole exceeded the digger's bailing rate. The cavity would then be lined with stones, bricks or tiles to prevent collapse and the opening often capped to prevent contamination and, indeed, theft of the precious water. Needless to say, this was arduous and dangerous work. Wells were also created by the insertion of a terracotta or wooden pipe into shallow water-bearing soils, usually of gravel or sand, or by excavating around existing springs, which would be tamed with stonework, bricks or a wall. In a sense wells represent the domestication of water.

The word 'well' is derived from the Old English *wiellan* 'to boil' or 'to bubble up', ie to 'well' up. And to go beyond etymology, it also means 'good' or 'in good health', physically, emotionally, spiritually, materially, or it can imply a degree of knowledge or closeness as in 'I know him well'. It can even be a rhetorical exclamation as in 'Well?' or 'Well, Well!'.

Lady's Well, Northumberland, is traditionally associated with St Ninian, who was known for his miracles, among them curing a chieftain of blindness. Lady's Well shows how wells and springs can be landscaped to become small lakes. Here the cross and garden bower make this site a place of contemplation.

The famous Winifrid's Well at Holywell in north Wales.

It has also come to mean a place where water has special curative properties. The beliefs that abound concerning wells are legion, with many wells credited with miraculous powers extending as far as divination. Hence the common appellation 'holy well'. Such wells often became shrines, and elsewhere in Europe holy wells still have very powerful followings, as at Lourdes in France. However, in Reformation Britain such places were increasingly regarded by Protestants as places of Papist idolatry and pilgrimage, even witchcraft. During the Commonwealth (1649–60) the Puritans were highly effective at outlawing well worship, a move from which the tradition never really recovered. The relationship of the Church to wells had in fact always been ambiguous. On the one hand, early Christian clerics were happy to tolerate the worship of so-called pagan spirits at springs, but later they were commanded to take over these shrines and replace the invisible Celtic spirit with a Christian saint, so offering both an immaculate pedigree of suffering and a virtuous curriculum vitae.

The only official ecclesiastical well site surviving in Britain is that at Holywell or Treffynon, a few miles from Flint in north Wales, still in use after 1,300 years and well attested historically. In his seminal work *Britannia* (first published in 1586, the first comprehensive topographical, geographical and historical study of Britain ever to be printed), William Camden had this to say about Holywell:

…there's a well much celebrated for the memory of Winifrid,
a Christian Virgin, ravished here, and beheaded by a tyrant…
Out of this well a small brook flows and runs with such violent
course that immediately it's able to turn a mill.

The date was AD660 and Winifred was on her way to see the chapel built by her uncle, St Beuno. The tyrant was a young chieftain called Caradoc. St Beuno came to the rescue and restored her head, or far more likely restored her, to consciousness. Winifred recovered and went into a nunnery, where she eventually became an abbess and, ultimately, a saint. And where her severed head supposedly fell, a spring appeared. The legend took root, and the rich and famous came to pay tribute, including Richard the Lionheart, who visited to pray for his Crusade, and Henry V, who came both before and after the Battle of Agincourt. Around 1490, a bath and spring house were built at Holywell by Margaret Beaufort, mother of Henry VII, and in 1774 the critic Dr Samuel Johnson paid a visit, remarking on the indecency of a young woman bathing there. History does not relate what happened to the bounder Caradoc, but Holywell became known as the 'Lourdes of Wales' and prospered from being on the pilgrimage route to Ireland and close to the Irish Catholic communities in Liverpool and Manchester. Sadly, things went awry in the early twentieth century when nearby mining operations affected the spring's output; 3,000 gallons per minute were reduced to a trickle and then to nothing. Today's pilgrims are treated to a spring fed by a municipal pipe, but the annual pilgrimage still takes place on 22 June, to coincide with midsummer.

Although many holy wells were linked to Christian saints and festivals, there is clear evidence of a much earlier worship of wells, predating the Roman invasion. One county which still has an abundance of Celtic holy wells is Cornwall, where there are over 190 recorded examples. Not all of these are actively worshipped in the real sense of the word, but they do exist and they are all documented. The Holy Well at Madron, near Penzance, is especially noted for its reputed powers of divination and cure. Much mention is made of certain cures at this well during the 1640s, later (1695) described in Camden's *Britannia* by the ecclesiastic and writer Edmund Gibson, and including one John Trelille:

> …a cripple who for 16 years together was forced to walk upon his hands by reason the sinews of his legs were contracted, was induced by a dream to wash in this Well, which had so good effect that himself saw him both able to walk and to get his own maintenance.

After this the well became 'superstitiously frequented' to such a point that:

> …the Rector of a neighbouring parish was forced to reprove several of his parishioners for it. But accidentally meeting a woman coming from it with a bottle in her hand, and being troubled with colical pains, desired to drink of it and found himself eased of that distemper.

Sadly, John Trelille's return to health was relatively short-lived, for he became a soldier and died in the English Civil War a few years later.

Until at least the 1930s the Holy Well at Madron was regularly visited by young unmarried women, seeking information on how many years of spinsterdom they were to endure before marriage. They would make crosses from two pieces of straw and drop them into the well. The number of bubbles that rose to the surface as a result served to indicate the number of years before she would marry. Still popular is the leaving of 'clouties', small pieces of coloured rag tied by visitors to trees and branches, lending a festive air to the immediate vicinity. This practice of making votive offerings stems from the belief that if one leaves a piece of clothing from next to the ailing part of the body, the ailment will disappear as the rag slowly disintegrates. It also explains why, traditionally at least, there was a certain reluctance to tidy up the wells. Pagan offerings or not, this is good old-fashioned sympathetic magic and not to be sneezed at. Who hasn't thrown a coin into a well and made a wish when no one was looking? Not all communities are relaxed about the ritual, however: in 1996, certain individuals offended by these 'heathen' practices cut down the branches on which the clouties were tied at Madron Well.

One feels that in many holy places where water springs forth naturally, Christianity has, for better or worse, muscled in on a much older belief system and, in so doing, pushed aside more ancient calendars and forms of worship. In the town of Glastonbury in Somerset, beneath the celebrated Tor, is found the Chalice Well, which, according to

The colourful rags of the Madron Cloutie well in Cornwall, named after St Madron, a Cornish hermit who died c.AD545. The rags, when placed next to an ailing part of the body, are reputed to cure the wound.

legend, is the last resting place of the Holy Grail – in which drops of Christ's blood were miraculously preserved. Combine that with Arthur, the Knights of the Round Table, Merlin, Lancelot, Guinevere and Avalon, and you have a powerful medieval concoction. The Chalice Well shaft was constructed in the thirteenth century and still delivers 25,000 gallons of water a day – of great use to the citizens of Glastonbury in times of drought. It is a place of healing, and there is a fine garden with old yew trees and one of the famous Glastonbury Thorns, allegedly the descendants of a hawthorn that sprouted from the place where Joseph of Arimathea (the uncle of the Virgin Mary) thrust his staff into a hillside overlooking Glastonbury. A sprig of one of these trees is traditionally sent to the Queen at Christmas time.

It is only in the last hundred years that most settlements in this country have had piped water. In many cases, its advent, at first only in the form of a single standpipe for the whole village, is within living memory. For centuries springs and wells were central to village life, the font of all gossip and the focal point for needs, tasks, thoughts and beliefs. How sad that today so many of these water sources are lost under concrete – piped, diverted, polluted and ignored.

Well ceremonies

One well tradition that does survive is centred on the limestone villages of the central and southern Peak District in Derbyshire. The origins of well-dressing ceremonies are unclear, but it is likely that they are pagan and connected with fertility, some villages even having a 'well queen'. The Romans were known to have dressed wells with flowers in worship of the goddess Fontanalia and certainly well-dressing was known in the years immediately after the Black Death of 1348–50, when certain villages attributed their salvation from plague to the local water (in actual fact, it is much more likely to have been due to their isolation). They paid thanks to their wells by 'dressing' them. Written records for Tissington go back to 1748, when Nicholas Hardinge, Clerk to the House of Commons, noted that 'at Tissington, Fitzherbert's village, we saw springs adorned with garlands'. Most ceremonies had died out by the 1950s. The celebrations at Tissington, however, continued unbroken except for the odd war, and foot and mouth disease (in 2001). With well-dressing actively revived in recent years for the local tourist industry, many thousands of people now descend annually on the well-dressing villages of the area – particularly Tissington, Wirksworth, Youlgreave, Tideswell and Eyam – for a succession of ceremonies through the summer.

The capped Chalice Well at Glastonbury. The ornate oak lid is based on a medieval design called *vesica piscis* (literally vessel of the fish), revived by Glastonbury archaeologist Frederick Bligh Bond in 1919.

Every summer over two hundred well-dressings take place in Derbyshire. Designs are created from flower petals and other natural objects like wool, parsley, straw, pumpkin seeds and coffee beans. These modern examples are from the 2002 Tissington festival.

The dressing of a well is a complex and skilled affair, and involves what is called 'petalling'. Great oak boards are soaked in the village pond and covered in a layer of moist clay. Petals of many different flowers, along with all sorts of other natural debris like wheat, leaves, black alder cones, bark, coffee beans, lichen, sunflower seeds, egg shells and feathers, are then used to decorate the boards, which are finally erected next to a well. The themes are often Christian, but sometimes depict such oddities as the birth of Enid Blyton, Tolkien's grave in Oxford, Mt Fuji, Lindow Man, local landscapes and land girls. These are extraordinary examples of folk art and as colourful as anything you might find in India. The completion of the well-dressing is signalled by a blessing from a cleric and then often a procession, especially in villages where there is more than one well to visit. A week of celebrations or 'wakes' often ensues, attended by many visitors; in 2002 at Tissington all six wells were blessed by the Bishop of Derby and 50,000 people visited the village in that week alone.

Another water ceremony that survived until 1830 was the Byzant or Bezant ceremony in Shaftesbury, Dorset. This ancient hilltop town had no real source of water of its own and so the inhabitants relied on four wells in Enmore Green at the bottom of Tout Hill. These were, however, in the demesne of the manor of Gillingham and so an offering was made each year to the steward of the manor. This became an elaborate ceremony where the Byzant or 'besom', as it was known, a kind of cornucopia with peacock feathers and garlands of gold, was paraded down Tout Hill, along with gifts of a calf's head, a pair of gloves, a gallon of ale and two penny loaves of wheaten bread. The ceremony was revived in 1972 and lasted into the 1980s but has, alas, been allowed to slip since then.

Hot baths, spas and bottled water

Not all wells were holy and pleasant, and indeed some of the hotter ones could easily be seen as works of the Devil. Take, for instance, the wells known as the Hell Kettles near Darlington:

> In a field belonging to this place, there are three great Wells of great depth, commonly called Hell Kettles, or the Kettles of Hell because the water by an Antiperistasis, or reverberation of cold air is hot in them. Men of better sense and discretion think them to have been sunk by an earthquake. That there are subterraneous passages in these pits and a way out of them was first discovered by Cuthbert Tunstall the Bishop who found a goose in the Tees which he had marked, and put into the greater of them for an experiment.

Such was man's curiosity about nature and geology. Little wonder, then, that some hot springs became spas – resorts of the wealthy and health-conscious. Some started out as Celtic shrines, like the hot spring of Sul in Bath, and Arnemetia in Buxton. Both were adopted by the Romans, becoming Aquae Sulis and Aquae Arnemetiae respectively. Both are in limestone areas where the water is pre-heated thermally more than a mile underground before emerging for the delight and delectation of its human audience. In Bath, the rainwater falls on the Mendips and surrounding hills, then sinks underground and re-emerges – pre-heated – in the middle of the tourist centre below. The rate of flow here is a respectable quarter of a million gallons a day at an impressive 46°C (115°F). The Celtic tribe the Dobunni were first here, holding the shrine of Sul. Little is known about how they worshipped the goddess Sul, but silver coins of this tribe have been found at the site. In the second half of the first century AD the Romans built a very substantial complex of baths and temples around the spring. They worshipped Sulis Minerva, and a beautiful bronze head of Minerva was discovered by workmen whilst digging for a new sewer in Bath in 1792. During Roman times the baths, the hot spring and the various temples were the very nerve centre of the city. Issues of the day, politics, philosophy and trade were all discussed, and physicians would have been on hand. Votive offerings and coins were thrown into the spring, as well as curses written out on sheets of lead. The spring was a multi-purpose centre, offering respite and cures from the ills and hard work of the world. It is extraordinary that so much should have survived.

When the Romans left, the main buildings collapsed, but the ruins were built over as part of a Saxon and, later, a Norman, monastery linked to the abbey. The hot springs remained in use and three new baths, whose origins were all Roman, were built. These were the King's Bath, the Cross Bath and the Hot Bath. After the dissolution of the monasteries under Henry VIII, the baths were kept in use and the curative powers of the waters extolled. Royal patronage encouraged the economic regeneration of Bath, which soon became a popular destination for the good, the great and the fashionable. The great travel writer, Celia Fiennes, was clearly impressed by England's oldest spa, as revealed in an extract from her *Early Journeys* (1685–96):

> At the sides of the arches are rings that you may hold by and so walke a little way, but the springs bubbles up so fast and so strong and are so hot up against the bottoms of ones feete…

And the benefits of lounging around in hot water were not lost on William Camden either, when he visited Buxton:

> There are nine springs of hot water, called at present Buxton well, which being found by experience very good for the stomach, the nerves and the whole body, the most Honourable George, the Earl of Shrewsbury, has lately adorned them with buildings and they begin to be frequented by great numbers of Nobility and Gentry.

from William Camden's *Britannia*, 1586

The bronze head of Minerva, discovered in Bath by workmen in 1792.

Buxton benefited hugely from its baths, with the Duke of Devonshire spending vast sums of money (gained from copper mining) in the construction of the crescent, the baths and an opera house, which still stands. During the eighteenth and nineteenth centuries, spa towns prospered across England, with Droitwich, Tunbridge Wells, Cheltenham, Clifton/Hotwells in Bristol, Leamington, Harrogate, Bakewell, Matlock and Ashby de la Zouch all competing for custom. Wales had its fair share, too, with Llandrindod Wells, Builth Wells, Trefriew near Conwy and the extraordinary Llangammarch Wells, which claimed to have the only drinkable barium spring outside Germany. Interestingly, it was discovered by a pig when the local river had run dry. In its heyday, during the late Victorian era, this small village, with a population of only a few hundred souls, boasted a pump room, golf course and fashionable links hotel, all now gone.

Spa towns were places for the upper and wealthier middle classes to relax, to mix, to be seen, to be cured, to enjoy the delights of food and gambling, to gossip, to find new husbands and wives. And in addition to ostentatious recreation and socialising, spa towns offered the opportunity to both luxuriate in the waters and to drink them. This was not always a pleasant experience. When Samuel Pepys bathed there in 1668 he met:

...very fine ladies; and the manner pretty enough, only methinks it cannot be clean to go so many bodies together in the same water...

from *Samuel Pepys's Diaries,* entry for 13 June 1688

When the economic depression hit after the First World War, many spa towns began to suffer, and the advance of medicine meant that illnesses were beginning to be understood more clearly and the appropriate treatments taken in hospital rather than in the spa. In addition, the development of Victorian household water systems meant that many people now had baths in their own homes. The real enemy of the spa, however, was the building of public baths, which made bathing available to all. Antibiotics, radiotherapy, swimming pools and jacuzzis have all worked against the spa, though it is interesting to see that water therapy is on its way back as a reliever of stress, and that spa-based holidays are now a huge boom area. In Bath, spa life has come full circle. In 1978, public bathing in the Beau Street Baths was stopped, when an amoeba was found in the water (which had come from an area of the earth's strata through which the water had passed), but now the old thermal baths have been restored, with an open-air, thermally-heated, rooftop swimming pool, therapeutic consulting rooms, and complementary and orthodox spa treatments. Just what the doctor ordered.

Relaxation, healing, gossip and gambling – spa towns offered a whole way of life for the wealthy, as depicted here at the Great Bath in Bath.

The restored spa will draw its water from the Hetling Spring, Cross Spring and King's Spring, receiving over one million litres (220,000 gallons) of water daily at a temperature of 45°C (113°F). This is a classic case of looking to the past for a vision of the future. Hydrotherapy, warm water, stimulation of the mind and body in the centre of a classic Georgian city.

In more recent years, of course, commercial marketing has seized the day and made mineral water both healthy and tasty. Malvern in Worcestershire, with nearly 90 recorded springs, and Buxton in Derbyshire have led the field. Some spa towns have preferred to stick to their medical laurels; the water in Harrogate, for example, is sulphurous and advised for lead and mercury poisoning, syphilis, anaemia and indigestion, among other ills. Leamington water is claimed to assist with scrofula, sciatica, haemorrhoids, jaundice and lymphatic glandular enlargements.

Meanwhile, bottling water at source is now a growth industry, booming – or rather sparkling – into the multi-million pound stratosphere. In this country, we consume approximately 1.6 billion litres of bottled water every year, and demand has tripled in the last decade. Two problems arise, however: the disposal of the plastic bottles and the

The Cross Bath today. Designed by Nicholas Grimshaw and Partners, the bath has been renovated as part of the Bath Spa Project.

distances that water travels. If you drink bottled water, drink local spring water and recycle the bottles. One good example is Kingswood Spring Water, pumped up from the chalk aquifer on the West Stourhead estate and then sold at all National Trust properties in the region, thus reducing transport costs. It is a sobering thought that bottled water in restaurants is sometimes one thousand times the price of tap water. People readily pay over £1 a litre for bottled water in a chic restaurant without batting an eyelid, and yet you can obtain 1 cubic metre of water through the humble tap for considerably less. Perhaps as a nation we are all too keen to bottle things up.

The Malvern Hills are home to over 90 recorded springs. Reservoirs, of course, have practical, recreational and aesthetic appeal.

Chapter Two

❖

**Streams of
consciousness**

PREVIOUS SPREAD **The gushing waters of the Afon Cwm Llan mountain river on the Hafod y Llan estate in Snowdonia.**

THE STREAM IN POETRY

Once the water leaves the precinct of the spring, it becomes a stream. Streams and rivers help define landscape, but the underlying geology is the main player. It gives the aquifer its level and resonance, which in turn determines the habits of a stream. If the rock is impervious – like granite – then the water table will be high and the stream will run off quickly, starting high up, as on upland peat moors. In the case of chalk, the aquifer will generally emerge at the foot of a hill or incline, where the limestone or chalk meets clay or another impervious rock such as green sandstone, and the water is able to break out. Rarely do streams start neatly. They are often just a series of indefinable oozes, producing a faint trickle that hardly seems capable of ever becoming a major landscape feature.

Let loose, the stream has the freedom to flow where it will. It is these early ripples, riffs and rills, these small chunterings, the sense of something growing, to which poets and artists are drawn. These impressions, glimpses of young boisterous streams, half seen, half heard and half tamed, are all deeply embedded in our minds. A mixture of wonder and movement, of anticipation and clarity that is part of the inner landscape, or the 'inscape', as Gerard Manley Hopkins called it.

The glistening thread of the River Kinder weaves its way down Kinder Scout in the Peak District.

Streams are great opportunists, and if conditions are right, then many will rise together. Dartmoor in Devon is an excellent place to see this in action: the Taw, Teign, Bovey, Dart, Avon, Erme, Plym, Walkham, Tavy, and the Lyd all start life on the moor. These acidic steams are often rumbustious in nature – in her recent book *Dart*, Alice Oswald refers to that Devon river near its source as 'a foal of a river', which then canters down to the sea. That streams have characters is also beyond dispute. Peaty streams, for example, can be dark and mysterious, whereas chalk streams are often crystal clear, emerging as small bubbling springs at the foot of green, well-grazed chalk downs.

Whatever their origin or character, streams lead us into and through the landscape in more than just a physical sense. It is always worthwhile seeing where such streams of consciousness lead. Certainly not always to the full blown river or the vast sea. Perhaps just to a daydream or rambling train of thought. Samuel Taylor Coleridge grew up beside the River Otter in east Devon, and was a poet clearly rooted in that landscape:

> *Dear native brook! wild streamlet of the West*
> *How many various-fated years have past,*
> *What happy and what mournful hours, since last*
> *I skimmed the smooth thin stone along thy breast*

> from *To The River Otter*

Maybe there is something small and innocent about a stream which makes it so appealing to the young and young at heart. Its infant qualities make it easy prey, certainly, to the poet. William Wordsworth spent his childhood with the Derwent, in a very close and tangible sense:

> *Was it for this*
> *That one, the fairest of all rivers, loved*
> *To blend his murmurs with my nurse's song,*
> *And, from his alder shades and rocky falls,*
> *And from his fords and shallows, sent a voice*
> *That flowed along my dreams?*

> from *The Prelude*

Yet the river not only lives on in his childhood as a romantic image, it gives a more important message, that solace may be found among the dismal images of the industrial revolution. Wordsworth continues:

> *For this, didst thou,*
> *O Derwent! winding amongst grassy holms*
> *Where I was looking on, a babe in arms,*
> *Make ceaseless music that composed my thoughts*
> *To more than infant softness, giving me*
> *Amid the fretful dwellings of mankind*
> *A foretaste, a dim earnest, of the calm*
> *That Nature breathes amongst the hills and groves.*

Streams are sometimes imbued with human qualities. In Tennyson's *The Song of the Brook*, we find a brook babbling at Somersby near Horncastle which is called the Lymn in its upper reaches…

> *I chatter over stony ways*
> *In little sharps and trebles*
> *I bubble into eddying bays*
> *I babble on the pebbles*

…but somehow becomes the Steeping lower down:

> *I chatter, chatter as I flow*
> *to join the brimming river*
> *For men may come and men may go*
> *But I go on forever*

Chattering, bubbling and brimming, streams always seem cheerful, bright and clear. It is a clarity that we wish to see reflected in our own thoughts and which can help us move towards a meditative state, absorbing sight, sound, taste, touch, even the smell of the water. Yet there is also a dark side, a hint of corruption and of torpor. Thomas Hardy lived beside the Stour in Dorset and left us this less than romantic – yet closely observed – verse about the footbridge in Sturminster Newton:

> *Reticulations creep upon the slack stream's face*
> *When the wind skims irritably past,*
> *The current clucks smartly into each hollow place*
> *That years of flood have scrabbled in the pier's sodden base*
> *The floating lily-leaves rot fast.*

> from *On Sturminster Foot-bridge*

Like half a river, half a poem, like Rupert Brooke – the poet cut off in his prime – these things stick in your mind precisely for being incomplete. Brooke, who no doubt spent many a languid hour punting up the Cam or tied up under willows reading poetry, writes about the 'yet unacademic' Granta which flows 'up' (or is it down) to Cambridge through Grantchester Meadows, expecting 'honey still for tea', yet tainted by decay and incipient tragedy:

> *Ah God to see the branches stir*
> *Across the moon at Grantchester*
> *To smell the thrilling-sweet and rotten*
> *Unforgettable, unforgotten*
> *River-smell, and hear the breeze*
> *Sobbing in the little trees*

> from *The Old Vicarage, Grantchester*

A path through the dramatic, foaming Devil's Cauldron at Lydford Gorge in Devon.

And here a second whiff of river movement, the sense of slow, yet powerful flow:

> *Oh, is the water sweet and cool*
> *Gentle and brown, above the pool*
> *And laughs the immortal river still*
> *Under the mill, under the mill?*

Here we are dealing with inner reflections, as did the Impressionists who so loved and mirrored the effects of light on water. Landscape remembered at a distance is always powerful, a place evoked by the rustle in the trees, the wind in the willows… Distance, solace, consolation. No surprise therefore, that these lines about Grantchester were in fact written many hundreds of miles away in a Berlin café in 1912, far from the source of Brooke's musings.

Vanishing streams

Now you see it; now you don't. The porous quality of chalk and limestone means that water will flow right through them with the greatest of ease, sometimes disappearing altogether when the flow is sluggish and given the chance to seep under. Some particularly fickle chalk streams dry up in summer and run only in winter. These waterways are known as winterbournes. In the Dorset valleys, a number of villages carry the prefix: Winterbourne Abbas, Winterborne Clenston, Winterborne Tomson, among others. In the Mendips of Somerset, lost or underground streams are called swallets, whilst in Derbyshire they go by the name of swallow holes and in Yorkshire ghyll or ghills, which can also be ravines and/or streams, as in Gaping Gill near Ingleborough. Some streams and rivers disappear only to pop up again, quite unperturbed, in a different place. For example, the Manifold and the Hamps rivers in Derbyshire both regularly disappear for several miles, usually in summer. The Manifold reappears at Ilam Park and flows on regardless, as if nothing had happened.

Even the Trent has been known to play this trick. In 1581 the vicar of Alrewas near Lichfield remarked (quoted in Camden's *Brittania*):

The water of the Trent dryed up so sodenly so ebb that I, John Falkner, vicar went over into hall meadow in the afternoone, in a low paire of shoes, about 4 of the clocke in the afternoone; and so it was never in remembrance of any man living in the droughtest yeare that any man had known, and the same water in the morning before was banke full, which was very strange.

Not all disappearing rivers are in the north, however. The River Mole in Surrey was well known for its vanishing acts, as Edmund Spenser attested:

> *Sullen mole that hides his diving flood*
> *Mole that like a nousling mole doth make*
> *His way underground, till Thames he overtake*

Underground streams and caverns played mightily on the imaginations of early man, inspiring him to paint the first masterpieces, with the themes of hunting by numbers, shamanic ritual or just a celebration. These first art galleries became rich hunting grounds for poets; two hundred years ago a visit to Cheddar Gorge and a few grains of opium gave us these memorable lines:

> *In Xanadu did Kubla Khan*
> *A stately pleasure-dome decree;*
> *Where Alph, the sacred river, ran*
> *Through caverns measureless to Man*
> *Down to a sunless sea.*

Coleridge had in fact visited Cheddar Gorge in 1794 with Robert Southey, and no doubt memories of it came flooding back to him whilst stuck ruminating in his armchair in a remote farmhouse on the edge of Exmoor. A vision which was sadly interrupted by the Gentleman from Porlock…

Waterfalls and cataracts

A sharp change in geology from hard to soft rock, or the emergence of an igneous dyke or a line of fault, will lead to sudden drops that spawn gorges, waterfalls, deep whirlpools and stretches of fast-moving rapids. These features were terrifying to early travellers, as is apparent in the comments of William Camden (from his *Britannia* of 1586) on the wilder parts of north-west Yorkshire. There is none of the wonder of these open spaces, so appreciated by later lovers of the picturesque. Instead there is only horror and awe:

> Where Richmondshire touches upon the county of Lancashire, the prospect among the hills is so wild, so solitary so unsightly, and all things so still, that the borderers have called some brooks that run here, Hell becks, that is to say Hell or Stygian rivulets; especially at head of the river Ure which with a bridge over it of one entire stone, falls so deep, that it strikes a horror upon one to look down to it. Here is safe living in this tract for goats, deer and stags which for their great bulk and branchy heads are very remarkable and extraordinary.

The same water in its wild and raw state later inspired Wordsworth, Coleridge and Southey. Indeed, the fast, tumbling rivers of the uplands were far more frequent a source of literary interest and general curiosity than their sluggish, lowland counterparts. Their dramatic character and spirit, especially impressive after heavy rain, certainly help explain this, but the intrigue is also due in part to the mythology associated with such places. Caves, caverns and subterranean waterways were traditionally regarded as home to supernatural figures, water sprites and fairies. Such figures could be both evil and benign, a potentially dangerous combination of beauty and treachery, and a direct

The stunning White Lady Waterfall at Lydford Gorge in Devon.

reflection of the appeal — and danger — of the river itself.

One of the most dramatic sequences of waterfalls in Britain is along the southern edge of the Brecon Beacons National Park in south Wales. A long band of limestone outcrop has created a beautiful and very particular landscape, characterised by wooded gorges, caves, swallow holes and waterfalls, fed by several rivers that drain the rain-fed mountains to the north (some of the wettest in Britain). Known locally as Coed y Rhaeadr, which strictly translated means 'Wood of the Waterfalls', although the area is known simply as 'Waterfall Country', the best falls are centred around the villages of Hirwaun, Ystradfellte and Pontneddfechan. Waterfalls in the south of England are much more rare than in Wales, but there is a particularly fine example at the National Trust's Lydford Gorge near Okehampton in Devon, where the river Lyd, fresh off Dartmoor, plunges down several hundred feet in little over a mile, via the deepest gorge in south-west England. At one end of the gorge is the spectacular whirlpool known as the Devil's Cauldron, while the dramatic White Lady Waterfall cascades down 27 metres (90 feet) or so at the other. The heavily wooded slopes between are rich in wildlife and interesting cultural associations; one stretch of the river downstream is even known as Pixie Glen.

The taming of the stream

Water may be essential raw material for poets, but having regular supplies of clean drinking water is of greater importance to the majority of us. A secure supply means the harnessing of water and its direction to the required point of delivery. The Romans — ingeniously — devised wonderful systems of 'man-made streams' for their towns, villas and army camps, featuring not just piped water and aqueducts but also sewers, some of which are still in use today. They chose the locations of their villas very carefully, the critical factor often being the needs of their farm animals: a cow will drink 60 litres (13 gallons) of water a day! Indeed, many droving routes were dependent not just on grazing but on ease of access to water. Negotiations between drovers and landowners often had to be made in advance. A day or two before the planned crossing, one of the drovers would go ahead and make an agreement with the landowner to dam up a stream, so that when the cattle arrived, there would be several hundred yards of bank where they could drink without stampeding to reach the crossing place. The cattle were often very thirsty and would rush down to the stream once they smelt it, and if there was a stampede, young cattle would be crushed and trampled and the bank of the river ruined. Advance negotiations were important in terms of setting a precedent with the landowner.

To be near a spring or small stream was therefore hugely advantageous; the density of Roman villas in Gloucestershire, for example, owes as much to geology and the emergence of springs and a pathway of streams as it does to the influence of the Fosse Way, the major Roman thoroughfare that connected Exeter with Lincoln.

The Romans used terracotta pipes to carry their water networks, but they were also adept at lead-working and opened up deep mining for lead in Derbyshire. The local lead ore was of high quality and once smelted was used to make highly efficient lead pipes and cisterns. Sheets of it were even exported to other parts of the Roman Empire. Lead and water became closely linked and, interestingly, it is from the Latin word *plumbum* for lead that we get the word 'plumber'. Lead was superior to terracotta or fired clay in the sense that it did not fracture, but it was expensive to produce and so not available to all. Wood was actually the most commonly used material for piping water, and wooden pipes were used right up to the nineteenth century. These were often bored out from trunks of elm or alder – both noted for their water-resistant qualities – with a hand auger, a tedious and exacting job. Bifurcations and connections could always be achieved by choosing a piece of wood with a branch or a 'Y' fork, and the pipes were tapered at the ends so they would slot into each other. They would then be fitted with a collar joint and sealed with pitch. Before assembly, the insides would have been charred from within to harden them and stop leakage.

The Roman skill of water management lived on in the religious houses, with many monasteries – especially those in rural areas – becoming very adept at using and manipulating water. A particularly fine example of a complex water system was developed at Fountains Abbey in North Yorkshire, where parts of the abbey were built deliberately over the River Skell. An advanced system of lead pipes and cisterns ran across the whole site, with sewers in place and the river used to keep the site clean and healthy. Just upstream was a corn mill, still in use in living memory and recently restored.

Managing water supplies alongside a river in an isolated and thinly populated area was one thing, but getting reliable supplies of water into the burgeoning towns of fifteenth- and sixteenth-century England was a much more challenging proposition. One

The extraordinary migratory journey of the salmon takes it up cataracts and waterfalls towards its spawning grounds.

The New River. Ceremony and pageantry went hand in hand with man's ingenuity in Sir Hugh Middleton's radical venture.

adventurous scheme to bring water into Plymouth was undertaken in 1589 under the direction of the city's mayor, Sir Francis Drake. A seven-foot wide leat or water-course was dug from the River Meavy at Burrator on Dartmoor for 17 miles – through difficult granite terrain – to Plymouth, which at that time had a population of 5,500. When the water was first introduced to the leat on 24 April 1591, a trumpeter announced its progress and the legend runs that Drake himself rode ahead of the torrent on a fine white horse. Public conduits were subsequently dug to channel the water into various parts of the city, and Plymouth relied on the leat for its water for much of the next three centuries. Parts of the original construction can still be seen today. Drake then had a monopoly on the mills in Plymouth and thus controlled the flour for shipping.

A similar scheme to Drake's was initiated in London in 1608. A long ditch – the 'New River' – was dug from Amwell near Ware in Hertfordshire into the very heart of the fast-expanding city of London. The scheme was devised and overseen by Sir Hugh Middleton, a wealthy goldsmith who began this great undertaking on 20 February 1608 and, as described by Walter Harrison in *A New and Universal History, Description and Survey of London and Westminster, Southwark etc*:

…with great difficulty, art, industry and expence cut a trench in some places full thirty feet deep, through oozy, muddy, stiff, craggy and stony ground, and with so many windings to find out a proper channel, that, from the fountain to the reservoir it measured thirty eight miles three quarters and sixteen poles.

Sir Joseph Bazalgette, mastermind of London's sewerage system.

Sir Hugh was ruined financially by the project (it cost him £500,000), but at least the 1613 opening was suitably spectacular:

On Michaelmas day 1613, Sir Hugh Middleton, Sir Thomas Middleton, his brother, with Sir John Swinnerton the lord mayor and many others went in grand cavalcade to the reservoir since called New River head. On their arrival, sixty labourers handsomely dressed in green caps, walked with their tools three times round the bason with drums and trumpets and after addressing the lord mayor in a copy of verses adapted to the occasion, the sluices were opened under the discharge of cannon, the sound of music, and the acclamations of all the spectators.

The New River was a phenomenal achievement, with no fewer than 43 sluices and 215 bridges, and proved to be of inestimable value to the city of London. However, the continuing expansion of the capital and growing population pressures meant that conditions in the city remained squalid and unsanitary. Many of the original rivers of London that had supplied the city with water in earlier centuries had by now become sewers rather than water-courses. In the eighteenth century, Alexander Pope had this to say about the Fleet:

where Fleet Ditch with disemboguing streams
Rolls the large tribute of dead dogs to Thames

from *The Dunciad: Book the Second*

and despite the efforts of earlier improvers, perhaps relatively little had changed in the capital since Andrew Boorde made his pertinent observations in *A Dyetary of Health* in 1542:

Beware of draughty privys and of pyssynge in draughts, and permit no common pyssyng place about the house – let the common house easement to be over some water or else elongated from the house. Beware of emptyng pysse pottes, and pyssing in chymnes

Unsanitary conditions bred disease and it was clear that if nothing were done the entire metropolis might sink into a sump of bilge and effluent. Attempts were made to improve the situation and by 1847 over 10 miles of earthenware glazed pipes were being sold each week in London. However, their introduction was not enough to prevent the 'Great Stink' of 1858, when the windows of Parliament had to be draped with curtains soaked in chloride of lime so that the honourable members could continue business. Clearly action was needed on several fronts. Edwin Chadwick had

The construction of the Fleet Street sewer, an engraving by Frederick Napoleon Shepherd (1819–1878).

already brought in his Public Health Act of 1848 and proof of the water-borne characteristics of typhoid and cholera led to a host of attempts to improve the quality of London's water, including the philanthropic provision of fountains and hand pumps. In 1859 Samuel Gurney founded the Metropolitan Free Drinking Fountain Association; the first of his fountains was erected near Smithfield and was soon being used by 7,000 people daily. The provision of fresh, clean water became a very Victorian crusade and many fortunes were expended in its pursuit. Alas, this was also the period during which many of London's rivers became lost from view, covered up or culverted in the battle against stench and disease. Foremost among these were the Fleet, the Tyburn and the Westbourne. The Serpentine was – and still is, albeit in different form – a key feature in Hyde Park. And at one time Knight's Bridge was just that.

Meanwhile, the subterranean engineering genius of Sir Joseph Bazalgette was responsible for the masterminding of London's sewers. He started work in 1859 and finished in 1865, having organised the construction of 83 miles of sewers underground, a system which was the envy of the world and is still in use after nearly 150 years. Amazingly, the network of Victorian sewers in London is currently proving very useful for certain state-of-the-art broadband companies that wish to insert their cables underground to reach houses and businesses without digging up the roads. Clean round the bend, a faint whiff of internet. All mod cons – Sir Joseph would have definitely approved.

Nineteenth-century London was not the only city with water problems. Between 1876 and 1891, demand for water in Birmingham doubled and the lack of an adequate supply was proving an obstacle to the city's further expansion. A remarkable long-distance scheme was therefore devised, by which water was brought from the Elan Valley in mid-Wales. Between 1892 and 1904 Birmingham City Council, led by Joseph Chamberlain, spent £6 million on pipes, dams and reservoirs, and on a 73-mile-long gravity-fed aqueduct. Two long syphons were built to get the water over the Wye and the Severn valleys, and some 50,000 workmen were involved in the whole project. Today, half of Birmingham's water still comes from the Elan Valley and, at a stately 2mph, takes 36 hours to get from its source near Rhayder to Birmingham. Interestingly, an earlier visitor to the Elan Valley was Percy Bysshe Shelley, who in 1811 walked all the way from Sussex to mid-Wales and stayed with his uncle Thomas Grove at Cwm Elan, a mansion later flooded by the reservoir. In his letters, Shelley describes the valley before the dam was built as 'rocks piled on each other to tremendous heights, rivers formed into cataracts by their projections, and valleys clothed with woods, [which] present an appearance of enchantment'.

Living on the dark side

Streams and rivers have a dark side. The idyll of Britain's natural waterways was often eclipsed by the rigours of the Industrial Revolution and this combination of eternity and darkness is a theme familiar to poets such as William Blake (1757–1827) who, rather like Wordsworth, sought solace in the clear water of the stream. In his *XII Song* he evokes memory, dalliance and love in the first verse and then moves abruptly at nightfall into an altogether darker mood:

> *I'll drink of the clear stream*
> *And hear the linnet's song;*
> *And there I'll lie and dream*
> *The day long:*
> *And when the night comes I'll go*
> *To places fit for woe*
> *Walking along the darkened valley*
> *With silent melancholy.*

Whether this was a personal problem or situation, or whether the dark satanic mills were already etched upon his mind when walking down the valley, is not clear, but the ambivalence is certainly there. It is an ambivalence that not only powered the Industrial Revolution but still haunts us in various ways. Streams and rivers which at one moment appear innocent can – within a few hours – become dark raging torrents, undermining banks, flooding fields and villages and drowning those who get caught in their grasp. Often it was the harnessing of the stream which led to the construction of mills and the growth of hamlets into towns. So in a sense the energy of the stream was the source of its own demise.

Waterways

The confluence of the Rivers Team and Tyne, photographed in 1985 by Trevor Ermel. Our rivers can so often become a dumping ground.

Streams become rivers, and rivers power trade and industry, the country's lifeline. They carried the brunt of the nation's traffic for hundreds of years, traffic that became increasingly more industrial. In stark contrast to the Thames, the rivers of the north-east of England – the Tees, Tyne and Wear – have witnessed their fare share of shipbuilding, heavy industry and chemical plants. The opening couplets of a modern poet's view of the River Team, which flows into the Tyne at Gateshead, do not shy away from the post-industrial world; rather they embrace it wholeheartedly for what it was – and is.

Who goes there? A scrap-yard river,
A brick-end, drowned-rat, rotten-wharfed river.

Where are you heading? Into the future,
Jiggering out the wastes of labour.

What do you carry? A shaft of nature,
Snaking its way through the neighbourhood factories.

Who are your allies? The dark starlings
That blacken the sky like iron filings

Over smoke stacks, gasometers, viaducts, tangles
Of rust-speckled dock leaves, and barbed wire brambles.

*Filthy old gut, what plagues do you spread
Through these derelict works?* I am memory's thread

How will you mend them? with hawthorn and rosehips
And fireweed, that burns and peels on the slag-heaps.

from *Team Gut* by Katrina Porteous

That we are now picking up the tab for short-term industrial gain is undisputed. The above words help convey the awful state of those rivers that have become entangled in industrial waste. They also outline the debt that we owe our silent rivers, and the legacy of industrial processes that cared little for the consequences of their actions. We can only hope that in an age of greater awareness and appreciation, the fate of our rivers can be improved and some of the worst victims rescued. As we shall see in Chapter Four, rivers have played a central role in our history and development, and they deserve our utmost respect.

Chapter Three

❖

Mills and waterwheels

WHEELS AND MILLS

Rivers and streams empower landscape in numerous ways. Over several thousand years, the process of clear felling woodland and enclosing the land slowly formed an essentially agricultural landscape – one which is still largely intact today. This new farmland not only enabled our ancestors to cultivate fields and grow their own food, but also was able to support much larger centres of population. By the Bronze and Iron Ages, agriculture had become more than a subsistence economy, and surpluses could be traded, both within Britain and with countries overseas.

The shift from being a 'hunter-gatherer' society to establishing settled agriculture raised various problems. One of these was how to grind down vast amounts of emmer and spelt – early forms of wheat – into flour in order that the growing populations could be fed adequately.

Initially, grinding was done by hand, using rotary querns. These were made of whatever hard stone could be procured locally; for example, in north Dorset many of the stones came from a small quarry at Pen Pits near Stourhead. Querns were usually about 18 inches in diameter and 3 inches thick, and anyone who has used one to grind flour for any length of time will know what hard work it is. No surprise, then, that considerable effort and initiative went into identifying alternative methods of grinding.

A drawing of a water-powered bellows from *Diverse et Artificiose Machine* by Ramelli (1558). Harnessing water power for stamps, hammers and bellows was vital for the iron industry.

PREVIOUS SPREAD Aberdulais Mill by J.M.W. Turner was painted 1796–7, and was based on a drawing he made during his third tour of Wales in 1795.

The watermill was the result. Quite who invented it is the subject of some debate; the Greeks, Syrians, Chinese, Egyptians have all laid claim. It might even have been the Persians, who developed sophisticated vertical axis windmills and *qanats* – long, underground water tunnels which could be used to power waterwheels. The simplest waterwheel is called the Greek or Norse mill. These are found today in the Himalayas and Afghanistan, working much as they would have done 2,000 years ago. Closer to home, they were still being used in Ireland and on the Isle of Lewis in the Outer Hebrides as recently as the late nineteenth century. These mills were probably called Greek mills because the first written reference to them is in Greek, and no doubt the Greeks perfected the design, for they had complex city-states to feed, and grinding grain by hand would have taxed the philosopher's mind. The term 'Norse mill' is used in Scotland, probably because the technology was introduced there by the Vikings during the eighth and ninth centuries AD.

Waterwheels have changed little since the *Luttrell Psalter*, created in the early fourteenth century. In the *Domesday Book*, written at the time of William the Conqueror, there were 6,000 mills listed.

Such simple mills were constructed with a vertical axis and so could be made out of a single tree trunk of about 12 to 18 inches in diameter. Seven blades or paddles were fitted to the axis at a slight angle and these were driven by a small chute or launder of water with about 6 feet of head, which came though the back of the mill. The top stone was connected to the trunk, and the bottom stone fixed into the floor of the mill, the whole apparatus being controlled by a wedge under the main post, which maintained the requisite distance between the two stones. These mills were also known as 'clack' mills because of the noise they made: a gadget called a damsel released the grain through the central hole every time the stone turned round, the grain falling – noisily – from a basket suspended above the hole.

The beauty of these mills was their simplicity. They could be set up on fairly insignificant streams and were small, low cost, and often individually owned and run. Location was paramount, as there had to be enough consistent water flow to guarantee a working supply. Too little and the mill would be useless for half the year; too much and the whole mill would flood, and the machinery be damaged. Convenience was the next prerequisite. Mills had to be either right in the middle of the village or town, or near enough to avoid unnecessary and tedious journeys by cart. One of the main problems was in the prime agricultural lands, ie in the valley floors, where rivers tend to be slow flowing. The only way sufficient head of water to drive a mill could be built up was by constructing millponds and weirs. A millpond would fill up at night, giving the miller six to eight hours' milling time the next day, once the gates were opened and the water was released. Some of the mills were tidal, and would create their own millpond with each high tide. Three Mills at Bromley-by-Bow on the River Lea in the East End of London is a very good example of this. The Isle of Wight

Grey wagtails are typical of rocky streams and rivers, but they also frequent weirs, bridges and millponds, and often nest in stone cavities.

Abandoned millstones at Longshaw, Derbyshire. Many of these stones would have been destined for river-barge travel. Cutting them required great skill and the texture of the stone was reflected in the quality of the flour.

also has several tidal mills, including one on Wootton Creek between Ryde and Cowes. Corn was transported here by barge from Southampton and the ground flour was distributed all over the island. Milling ceased in 1945, and the mill was demolished in 1962. However, a few tidal mills do remain in the world, one of them being Eling Tide Mill on the Solent, where the power of the tide is still harnessed for the regular production of flour.

Once the location for a watermill had been chosen, the construction of the mill itself took great skill and was an expensive business. No great surprise, then, that many early mills were owned by a feudal lord or a monastery, by far the most reliable sources of capital. Millwheels were usually made of oak or elm, the cogs of elm or apple wood.

Stones were made out of gritstone, granite or 'pudding stone'. The latter is a very hard conglomerate found in the Chilterns. Most popular of all was the stone known as 'millstone grit', a type of sandstone found in the eastern Pennines. Choosing the right sort of stone was imperative and good-quality millstones were much in demand, and dispatched far and wide.

Increasingly, water was power. By the end of the seventeenth century there were approximately 20,000 watermills in England and almost every reasonably sized town – and many villages – had their own. Mills were a vital part of the local economy and much time and energy was invested in their construction, maintenance and development. Not surprisingly, there were strict regulations about their use, down to which mill one had to go to. Supplies of water were tightly controlled anyway, not least because water was often used for purposes other than grinding corn. For example, during medieval times it provided power for the small blast furnaces used to smelt iron, particularly across Kent, Sussex and Surrey. On the edge of Dartmoor, such furnaces were also known as 'blowing houses', because the water-turned wheels operated powerful leather bellows which gave a continuous blast of air.

The smelting season usually ran from October to April. This was because continuous high heat was essential in the furnaces and this could only be achieved when there was water enough to power them, i e, during the wetter times of the year. In drier parts of the country, seasonal water shortages meant that holding ponds had to be constructed, sometimes fed only by small springs. However, recent excavations and working reconstructions at Rievaulx Abbey in Yorkshire show that some of the remote northern monasteries, with easy access to constantly abundant water supplies in local rivers, were able to develop large-scale blast furnaces, an early example of water power as a driving force in the evolution of industry. Water also powered a host of other machinery, much of which was central to economic life – both locally and nationally. By the twelfth century, waterwheels were already being used to drive fulling mills (fulling being part of the cloth-making process), and the woollen industry gradually moved from traditional guild towns in the east of the country to areas of higher rainfall in the north and south-west, where the mills were increasingly concentrated. The eighteenth-century development of the Irish linen industry was overwhelmingly dependent on water-powered mills, with many being set up on the rivers around Belfast in particular. One of these – Wellbrook Beetling Mill, now in the care of the National Trust – has been restored to working order. Its huge hammers, which pound the cloth to give it the required linen sheen (the 'beetling' process), are driven by water carried on a wooden aqueduct from a weir on the Ballinderry river.

Increased mechanisation in agriculture demanded a range of metal tools and equipment. The mills responded accordingly, often specialising in particular types of implement. In Ireland, for example, the dependence on turf as a source of domestic fuel created strong demand for turf-cutting spades. Today, however, Patterson's Spade Mill near Templepatrick in County Antrim is the last water-driven spade mill in the country, although its machinery remains intact and spades are still being made there. Equally, the village of

Sticklepath, on the River Taw near Okehampton in Devon, was once home to a thriving water-powered industry which produced agricultural implements, as well as hardware for the local mining industries. The only surviving evidence of Okehampton's industrial past is the National Trust's Finch Foundry, still in working order.

Watermills were also used in the production of gunpowder. Among the first water-powered gunpowder mills were the Chart Mills at Faversham in Kent, established around 1560 and functioning until the 1930s (when the banning of gunpowder in mines virtually killed the industry). They have since been restored and are now open to the public. Water was ideal for powering gunpowder mills because of the obvious risk of sparks from other power sources, but even so, it was a highly dangerous occupation. For this reason, gunpowder mills were often constructed in remote locations, such as at Powdermills in the middle of Dartmoor, with the buildings well spaced out and 'blast banks' constructed to help confine the impact of any explosion.

As Britain's economic development strengthened through the seventeenth and early eighteenth centuries, some mills grew to become fairly extensive premises, precursors to the later 'manufactories' of the Industrial Revolution. Mill architecture was a building form all of its own, an amalgam of storage and warehousing with a functional mill, together with a mill house for the owner (or, increasingly in later years, the manager), who had to be on hand at all times. A good example of this type of complex is the National Trust's Houghton Mill near Huntingdon in Cambridgeshire. The mill, the largest on the river Great Ouse, was owned in the Middle Ages by the Benedictine abbey of Ramsey, 10 miles away. The abbey levied a tax – known as multure – on the flour ground at the mill, which in its heyday ran ten pairs of stones powered by three separate waterwheels. The present building dates from the eighteenth century and was extended in the nineteenth. It was a building of some sophistication and even had a water-powered ventilation system. Today the mill is notable for its specially designed propeller turbine, which produces hydroelectric power not only for the mill but also for the National Trust's nearby Wicken Fen Nature Reserve.

Watermills were flexible, too. As market requirements changed and evolved, so mills responded. There are plentiful examples of cornmills being converted to sawmills, for instance. Mills were also essential for pumping, whether to divert water out of a river for domestic use, as from the Thames in London, or for activities such as mining. Their flexibility became especially important to Britain during the second half of the eighteenth century, with the advent of the Industrial Revolution placing water power firmly at the cutting edge of this period of huge economic and social change.

The birth of cotton mill culture

The first one hundred years of the Industrial Revolution were powered primarily by water. In fact, one can be even more specific and say that it was in the steep-sided, water-abundant valleys of Derbyshire, Lancashire and Yorkshire that the rapid transformation of Britain into an industrial society really began. Apart from horsepower, water power became the main power source in society, and was infinitely more significant in terms of its impact on the nation's economy. The expansion of overseas trade during the seventeenth and eighteenth centuries fuelled a spirit of optimism and adventure among scientists and engineers. It was a revolution which did not just speed up machinery for wool and cotton processing, but which accelerated social change on a scale the world had never seen before.

In some places the landscape changed beyond all recognition. Quiet, wooded valleys suddenly became home to canals, mills and factories, with rows of purpose-built terraced housing (and, later, whole towns) springing up out of nowhere. One important example of the role of waterpower in this transformation was at Cromford in Derbyshire, where Richard Arkwright, a native of Lancashire and a wigmaker by training, developed his first cotton mill and spinning frame in 1771. This he did with Jedediah Strutt, who owned a large silk hosiery and knitting business in Nottingham. Arkwright chose Cromford because, unlike most mills, it provided not only the water from the millstream, in this case

Imposing and brooding, Houghton Mill on the River Ouse in Cambridgeshire is a powerhouse of ingenuity.

the Bonsall brook, but also a surfeit of underground water from Cromford Sough, an adit which drained several local lead mines. There was therefore a constant flow of water at a temperature which was always above freezing. Aware of the value of the site, Arkwright built his mill in a narrow gorge, over which it was relatively straightforward to control access and protect his endeavours.

Arkwright had to do most of his experiments on machinery behind closed doors – he was quite rightly concerned about other businessmen purloining his ideas. His 'water frame' was a machine for spinning cotton thread evenly, a task which had always been done by hand. Output from his new machine was enormous and banks of the water frames were soon made and housed in buildings designed specially for the purpose. These buildings had many windows, so maximum light fell on the machines (allowing workers to continue for longer and productivity to rise). High walls were built around the mill (and can still be seen today), spawning a new type of 'fortified mill architecture'.

Arkwright also pioneered the building of hostel accommodation, and built the village of Cromford to house his workers. By the standards of the day, they were well looked after, and on holidays were given beer, buns and brass bands.

Arkwright's mills were the wonders of the newly industrialised world. In 1790, Viscount Torrington had this to say about Cromford:

…these cotton mills, seven stories high, and fill'd with inhabitants, remind me of a first rate man of war; and when lighted up, on a dark night, look luminously beautiful…

A view of the Cromford Mill complex today, built by Arkwright between 1771 and 1790. It was the world's first successful water-powered cotton mill.

Yet Arkwright was only one of an increasing number of mill owners, and his mill designs were soon expanded upon and repeated over and over across the country. By the 1780s, mills were springing up all over the Midlands and parts of the north. One very fine example of a large, five-storey mill can be seen at Quarry Bank Mill, at Styal in Cheshire. Here, water-powered weaving still takes place, the water being harnessed from the Bollin River. The mill was constructed in 1784 by Samuel Greg, whose family had come from Belfast via Manchester, and the mill and its accompanying village, specially built for the mill workers and complete with school, shop and chapel, give a fascinating insight into the working and living conditions of the day. The mill had a hundred or so apprentices, both boys and girls, aged between seven and twenty-one and making up to one third of the total workforce. They were housed in the Apprentice House, built in 1790, and worked every day from 6am to 8.30pm, with three short breaks during the day. They were paid minimal or no wages, and many of them came either from the workhouses of Liverpool

The pediment over the mill door at Quarry Bank, showing Samuel Greg's inscription.

or were indentured from poor local families. Life was hard, although Quarry Bank Mill ran a less harsh regime than many other mills, and life expectancy there was better: fatalities per year were seven per 1,000 workers, compared to 33 per 1,000 in Manchester. The mill was given to the National Trust in 1939, and although none of the original machinery survives, the giant waterwheel still powers looms, spinning a coarse calico similar to that manufactured during the mill's heyday.

Whatever economic benefits accrued from the development of the mills and their products, the social aspects were generally much less positive. During the second half of the eighteenth century the 'enclosures' were beginning to take their toll and many people were effectively thrown off the land. Facing destitution, they drifted to the new towns in search of work. The mills did at least offer some opportunity for a livelihood, but the conditions in many of them were little short of appalling. Long hours, child labour and mistreatment were the norm. Accidents were commonplace, and the vast array of noisy machines made speech almost impossible, workers having to learn to lip-read to communicate with each other. The atmosphere in the mills was always kept hot and humid so that the threads would not break, and as the number of workers increased, so conditions in their towns and villages deteriorated. In many senses, they had exchanged one type of destitution for another, and this soon moved social reformers such as Jeremy Bentham, Thomas Malthus and John Stuart Mill to think about the world which was unfolding in front of their eyes. This state of affairs ultimately led to social reforms and re-adjusted political and economic thinking. A whole host of legislation was introduced between 1833 and 1850 to improve the lot of mill- and factory workers. Interestingly, Frederic Engels mentions Quarry Bank Mill and Samuel Greg in his book *The Conditions of the Working Class in England* (1844).

This was a time of social revolution, powered by water and ingenuity. Waterpower and its industrial applications had unleashed great financial wealth and unpredictable social forces, both of which helped shape the future of Britain. The movers and shakers of the Industrial Revolution, even though they often had rough edges and brusque manners, were highly ingenious inventors and successful businessmen, and became well connected and well respected. The wealth of the country rested on their shoulders – and was being generated in their water-powered mills.

Hydroelectricity and water-powered funiculars

As the nineteenth century unfolded, waterpower was adapted by the resourceful Victorians for more sophisticated uses. For example, water energy was increasingly harnessed to produce electricity through hydroelectric schemes. This form of power generation required a constant head of water and a turbine and when, in 1879, Joseph Swan invented the incandescent electric lamp, Sir William Armstrong (an inventor and businessman) was so fascinated by the new creation that he installed a turbine and a series of man-made lakes and underground pipes at his new house, Cragside, near Rothbury in Northumberland. The following year, Cragside became the first house in the world to be lit by hydroelectricity, 'the palace of a modern magician' as one contemporary account described it. Hydraulics and special bevel gearing also powered a spit in the kitchen and a lift to the upper floors. Hydraulic engineering was Sir William's forte; he had already created the swing bridge over the Tyne, in use since 1876. Newcastle was his city, and became the first town in England to use electricity for public lighting. Paris followed suit. Now in the care of the National Trust, Cragside remains a byword for Victorian ingenuity, with much of Armstrong's epic engineering efforts still on view today in and around the house.

The front elevation of Quarry Bank Mill, showing the uniformity of the imposing red-brick building.

The River Dulais gushes over
the rocks and boulders at
Aberdulais Falls.

Meanwhile, at Aberdulais, near Neath in West Glamorgan, the swift waters of the River Dulais have been powering waterwheels for over 400 years. In the eighteenth century, Aberdulais boasted an iron works, a corn mill and a fulling mill, and was very much at the heart of the Welsh industrial revolution. Today, something of the site's tranquil quality has been restored, but the natural waterfall still supplies over 200kw of electricity via a turbine, whilst a reconstructed waterwheel generates 25kw and is currently the largest waterwheel used in Europe to produce electricity. One of the most intriguing uses of waterpower at Abderdulais is the hydraulic fish lift which, thanks to the waterfall, allows salmon and sea trout access to the upper reaches of the river, otherwise out of bounds.

One of the great inventions of the Victorian age was the water-operated funicular railway. Thirty were constructed in total, and twenty are still operating today. The concept was inspired by the quarry incline railways, such as the Portland Merchants Railway in Dorset or that at Prior Park in Bath, which was horse-drawn, constructed in order for building-stone to be brought down to the River Avon and transported on. Water-powered funiculars were simple, effective and efficient, and worked on the basis of two counter-balancing cars or carriages, in which passengers would travel. The descending car would be water-ballasted, so pulling up the ascending one. Adjustments in the amount of water required would be made according to how many passengers were in each car.

The Victorians soon saw the potential of this exciting new mode of water-powered transport, both in practical and recreational terms. During the last two decades of the nineteenth century, many funiculars were constructed, linking piers, promenades, arcades and scenic walks in coastal towns like Aberystwyth, Hastings, Bournemouth, Scarborough, and Lynton–Lynmouth, one of the longest and steepest of those still operating today. Others were constructed inland, such as at Bridgnorth on the Severn, and served the more practical function of moving heavy goods, as well as people, to the top of the town. Funiculars became part of the national public transport system, as with the Clifton Rocks Railway in Bristol, which connected the river steamers on the Avon with the fashionable hotels of Clifton, above the Avon Gorge. This railway, constructed entirely within the cliff, was opened in 1893 and ran along a 152-metre (500-foot) tunnel at a gradient of more than one in two. Despite its early popularity, it was making a loss by the late 1920s and closed in 1934, although the tunnel was used by the BBC during the Second World War. The derelict railway buildings stand as a reminder of the heyday of Victorian water power.

Chapter Four

❖

Old man river

NAMING THE RIVER – THE LANGUAGE OF FLUIDITY

Rivers have always been mysterious. They play hide and seek, conveying many messages and speaking their own fluid language. We have to interpret their often mischievous and unpredictable ways. Rivers have their own culture, one which we have sought – often in vain – to suppress and control. Physically powerful, they are able to breach their banks and destroy bridges, and flood towns and farmland. And they can also be vehicles of human power, both political – serving as defences and boundaries – and economic, fulfilling a major historical role as trade routes and providing opportunities for commerce. In the same way that they divide and join with other waterways, rivers serve to both separate and unite people. They are a central linking factor in all our lives, and one that we have constantly sought to control. No surprise, then, that they are worshipped, feared and celebrated.

River names are among the most ancient in existence. Most are Saxon or Celtic, whilst others are of French or Scandinavian derivation. The Celts in particular worshipped and venerated springs, wells and rivers, and many of the names they gave rivers were probably related to the particular god or goddess they believed to live there. Some rivers were sacred, had several names bestowed upon them, and in some instances could only be referred to indirectly. Understanding the origin and meaning of river names is a perilous art, and many scholars have burnt the midnight oil over medieval manuscripts trying to trace names back to their source. The great tome *English River Names* was written by a Swede, Eilert Ekwall, and first published in 1928. This remains the standard work of reference on the subject, and it is fascinating to see how river names have developed to reach the names accepted by today's Ordnance Survey. River-naming is an evolving art; some rivers change name en route to the sea, others operate two names anyway, such as the Thames and the Isis, or as in Dorset with the Piddle and the Trent. Two river names can also be combined in a single place-name, eg Piddletrenthide (a hide being a medieval measure of land). Quite often, learned men such as John Leland, Henry VIII's librarian, or William Camden (see p.16) in the sixteenth century were the first to record river names and invariably their versions have stuck. Even so, many smaller streams have yet to be properly recorded or named.

Names for large, powerful rivers have often survived for thousands of years and become part of our language at a very deep level. The Ouse, Frome, Trent, Kennet, Severn, Exe, Tees, Don, Dee, Taw, Lune, Calder and Wye, for example. The list is seemingly endless and contains some of the most magical sounds in our language. Other names have clear Saxon origins, often featuring the words 'bourne' or 'burn', such as Ashbourne and Otterburn. In the north-west and the north-east of England, meanwhile, there is clear evidence of large-scale Scandinavian settlement. Here, place-names featuring the words 'beck', 'rill' and 'dale' are common. Even the odd French name crops up, as in Hampshire's Beaulieu River, harking back to Norman times.

PREVIOUS SPREAD **The River Lathkill in the Peak District National Park, Derbyshire.**

As for the actual meaning of these odd-sounding names, Avon or Aune simply means river: Afon in Welsh, Aven in Breton, Abann or Abhann in Irish (as with the River Bann,

which flows into and out of Lough Neagh). In England, there are several River Avons, including the Hampshire Avon, which meets the Dorset Stour at Christchurch, for which the old name was Twynham or Thuinham, meaning 'where two waters end or meet'. There is also the Gloucestershire Avon, which rises at Tetbury, winds through Wiltshire and then through Bath, Bristol and Avon Gorge, under Brunel's Clifton Suspension Bridge, to emerge finally at Avonmouth. Shakespeare's Avon at Stratford flows on to join the Severn at Tewkesbury. Then there is the Dartmoor Avon, the New Forest Avon and yet another Avon near Berkeley in Gloucestershire. Stour is a common river name, such as the Dorset Stour, which rises at Stourhead. Although its meaning is not certain, according to Ekvall it may denote the 'strong, powerful one'. There are further Stours in Worcestershire and Kent, as well as the Essex/Suffolk Stour, immortalised by Constable.

Constable's *Boys Fishing* ('A lock on the Stour'), *c*.1812. Such locks were vital for inland navigation, for example to take grain down to the Thames barges and thence to London, and to bring back coal which had travelled down the east coast from Newcastle.

A river's name is often derived from Old English or Celtic words related to its size or character. In *Rivers of Britain* (1986), Richard and Nina Muir highlight some examples:

Current name	Celtic name	Meaning
Clyst	cloust	cleansing one
Eden	ituna	gushing
Frome	fram	fair river
Kennet	cunetio	regal or holy
Taf	tamos	water
Test	trest	swift, strong
Ure	isura	holy
Wey, Wye	wey	flowing

Some rivers are associated with, and named after, trees. Ekvall again:

Alder: Wearne and Warren Burn
Ash: Ann and Onny
Elm: Leam, Lemon, Lymn and Lympne
Hazel: Cole
Oak: Darent, Dart and Derwent
Yew: Iwerne

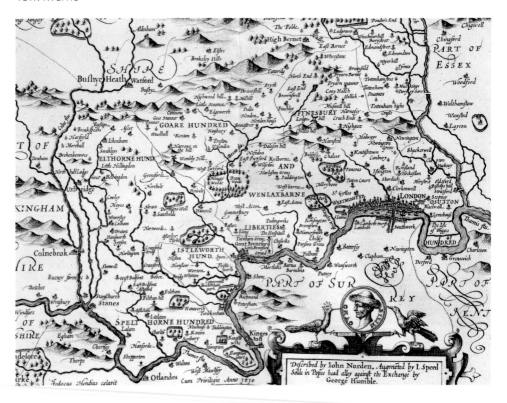

Speed's Map of Middlesex showing London in 1611, with London Bridge as the only crossing point. This map, a tribute to the skill of the early mapmakers, clearly shows many of the rivers and streams of the area, now hidden under urban sprawl.

Rivers as boundaries

Since time immemorial, large rivers have been used as divisions between tribes and counties, delineating spheres of influence, rights to hunting, even language and trade. At the same time, rivers connect people and places, providing both emotional and physical access. Yet there is an ambivalence about rivers that makes them both a help and a hindrance. They are certainly effective as defensive boundaries. In Saxon times, for example, the Thames served as the boundary between Wessex and Mercia. Equally, in the seventh and eighth centuries, the River Parrett in Somerset was taken as the boundary between the Saxon and the Celt. This later shifted west to the Tamar which, to the ardent Cornishman, is an international boundary, defined by Athelstan in AD936, who as a Saxon king tired of the wrecking habits, warlike raids and intemperate attitude of the Cornish, decided to clear Devon of the indigenous British. The decreed boundary was the eastern bank of the Tamar, so the salmon that are netted to this day are in fact Cornish speaking…Today the Tamar is still regarded as a linguistic, cultural and economic boundary.

Local identity is often defined by the name of a river and its course to the sea. Without written language or maps, rivers and catchment areas provided convenient demarcations. The maps of John Speed, published in his atlas *Theatre of the Empire of Great Britaine* (1611), are superb examples of human topography, of a truly living landscape, and they give a wonderfully clear picture of our rivers and of why our county towns and boundaries are located where they are. Location, location, location… but one determined by rivers and crossing places, fords and bridges, rather than by railways and motorways.

Coracles are still used on some Welsh rivers, such as the Teifi (for salmon netting). The net is strung out between two coracles that race downstream and then bring the net skilfully to shore, hopefully with a captured salmon or two.

Osier-cutters enjoying tea and toast by the fire on Chiswick Eyot, an island in the Thames, in 1927. Osiers were often used to make baskets for fruit-picking.

Even in relatively recent times, rivers have been involved in political controversy. As part of the local government reorganisation in the early 1970s, a whole host of new counties were created, based on the drawing together of opposing sides of major rivers; Avon, Humberside and Merseyside are just three examples. There are also examples of rivers as ancient boundaries, however, such as the Bristol Avon between Gloucestershire and Somerset. Monmouthshire is a county defined on three sides by rivers, with the Wye as a boundary with Gloucestershire and the Forest of Dean; the Rhymney with Glamorgan; and the Monnow with Herefordshire.

Rivers and access

Since the earliest times rivers were used by humans to move both themselves and their goods from place to place. Almost every part of lowland Britain was accessible to small hide-bound boats or rafts with a draught of no more than 80 centimetres (2 feet 6 inches). Initially, trade and exchange took place between neighbouring tribes, with displays of wealth and status developing into a language of diplomacy, a forging of reciprocal bonds which led to co-operation rather than to antagonism. Although rivers were the key to resupply, trade was as much a social occasion as an opportunity to barter surpluses. An idea of the cultural wealth of the Iron Age can be gauged by the rich finds unearthed at the lake villages of Glastonbury and Meare in Somerset; it has been suggested that this was where three tribes, the Dobunni, the Durotriges and the Dumnonii, met to trade at certain times of the year.

However, not all meetings on, or next to, rivers were friendly. The fact that rivers often offered the fastest way of penetrating unknown or foreign territory was not lost on the Romans, for example, who, at the time of their invasion of Britain under the Emperor Claudius in AD43, used river valleys as one of their main means of access across England. This was particularly so in the east of the country, and was a technique emulated several hundred years later by the Vikings, who sailed their longboats well inland and even as far as the town of Thetford in Norfolk, at the very heart of East Anglia. This strategy was not based purely on criteria related to ease of access. The fact that almost all inland settlements of any size (and the most productive agricultural land) were located along rivers meant that a river-borne approach was often the most effective way of striking a blow at the local population. Rivers were the lifeblood of most parts of the country, and the appearance of the enemy on them was certain to cause a degree of panic, both physical and psychological. Once the enemy was able to dominate river traffic and river banks, the game was as good as over.

As well as providing a means of moving from place to place, rivers also constituted a source of livelihood for many thousands of people. River products – ranging from rushes to fish to watercress (see Chapter Six) – could be harvested and used, eaten or sold. Although many river inhabitants led highly sedentary lives – living, working and dying only feet from the water's edge and often operating at little more than subsistence level – the most entrepreneurial and successful of them branched out, using the river, its harvest and its opportunity for transportation to become involved in trade.

River towns and trade

Extensive river trade in Britain goes back to at least the Bronze Age, and the remains of large boats dating back to 1500BC have been found in the Humber, already a major thoroughfare by that time. Water-borne goods were sometimes of monumental proportions, such as the vast stones required for the creation of Stonehenge and brought to Salisbury Plain from the Preseli Hills of south Wales by river, sea and then river again. River towns and inland ports were well established by medieval times and served as the backbone of the local (and, in many cases, regional) economy for centuries. For much of that time, the prosperity of these settlements depended on the river, each town's commerce ebbing and flowing with the water. Fluidity like liquidity, trade and profit, which both brought and required an architectural infrastructure: wharfage, staiths, hythes and warehouses.

River settlements soon became more than simply a collection of buildings along the banks. Nearly all of our county towns are situated at crossing places on important rivers, where early fords and ferry points were replaced by permanent bridges. Many of these sites were established and developed by the Romans, who built garrison towns at strategic river crossings and road intersections. This was the basis of a

Lesser pond-sedge is one of several species of sedge and rush that were traditionally used by river folk to make objects as diverse as baskets and light tapers.

A drawing by J.P. Hunter of the North Brink of Wisbech in Cambridgeshire, August 1840. The small river barges in the foreground would have taken cargoes up the River Nene to Peterborough via the Dog-in-a-Doublet lock.

national network, much of which we retain to this day. Saxon towns often followed on from the sites of their Roman forebears, and these in turn were reorganised and fortified by the Normans after their conquest in 1066. Stone for their many castles (and also for the proliferation of church-building that took place at this time) was moved extensively by water, on river barges. Many small settlements evolved into inland ports, rich trading centres which in turn became political and ecclesiastical seats of power, fully equipped with cathedrals and abbeys, High Sheriffs and Lords Lieutenants, county courts and county councils. River trade was vital; 95 per cent of Reading's trade came by river, before the advent of the railways in the mid-nineteenth century.

Some of these medieval river towns became free ports, English versions of the small independent city-states so widespread elsewhere in Europe. Bristol, Exeter, Bridgwater, York and Lincoln all prospered in this way. With growing trade in lucrative commodities such as wool and wine, these river ports flourished, each with its own area of specialism and proud of its trade with the Baltic, France, Spain and Italy. Wisbech is an excellent example of a successful inland port. In Saxon times it was actually on the coast, where the River Ouse entered the Wash. Today it is 12 miles inland and on the River Nene! Siltation, changes of river course, new coastal defences, as well as the pumping and reclamation of farmland have all changed the landscape. The surrounding peat has dried up and sunk, and the rivers are now higher than the land. A major East of England river, the Nene is 90 miles long and navigable not just to Peterborough (some 30 miles or so upstream from Wisbech) but as far as Northampton, where there is a link to the Grand

Union Canal. Wisbech, therefore, had an enormous hinterland and was connected to the industrial Midlands by a series of canals. Between 1805 and 1825 the port trade doubled from 30,000 to 70,000 tons a year, with almost everything coming and going by water. At times there were up to 40 sailing vessels either at dock in the port or moored up waiting to unload. Much of Wisbech's trade was with Holland and the Baltic, and there were many Hanseatic warehouses in the town. Goods varied widely from furs and skins to cattle, grain, wool, soft fruit and potatoes. Coal, brought in colliers from Newcastle and Sunderland, was used to fuel the pumping engines that drained the surrounding fenland. Many a fortune was made in Wisbech, and this is reflected in the elegant and opulent houses that line the town's waterfront, including Peckover House, now in the care of the National Trust.

Wisbech was the birthplace of Octavia Hill, one of the founders of the National Trust. She was born in a house on the banks of the Nene in 1838, and her father's family had extensive corn trading, transport and brewing interests. The Hills also owned the packet boat services that ran between Wisbech and Peterborough. Octavia's parents were champions of the poor, setting up evening classes for the labourers in the warehouses and helping workmen to pool their money to buy land and become 'free'. Octavia went to London when she was two, but the early days of her parents' social reform work in the thriving port of Wisbech must have left a deep impression on her, and one that helped form the values she pursued so vigorously in later years.

A contemporary view of Peckover House on the North Brink. The wealth to be derived from shipping is clear to see from the elegance of the merchants' houses.

A map of the Navigations by the Rivers and Canals of West London (1787–1811), showing the endeavours of the early canal-builders and their desire to connect the Severn with the Thames. The map also shows a series of interesting short canals in south Wales, built to bring coal down to the sea ports.

The River Thames and London

Sweet Thames, run softly, till I end my song.
The river bears no empty bottles, sandwich papers,
Silk handkerchiefs, cardboard boxes, cigarette ends
Or other testimonials of summer nights. The nymphs have
departed.

from *The Fire Sermon* by T.S. Eliot (1922)

The most successful river port of all was London, nourished and sustained by the Thames. The river runs for some 215 miles from its source in Gloucestershire through the soft underbelly of England, past Oxford and Reading to its estuary into the North Sea. Rather like nineteenth-century wrangles over the source of the Nile, the debates about the source of the Thames continue. Some say it is at Seven Springs near the village of Coberley, south of Cheltenham, where an inscription in Latin declares *Hic tuus o tamesine pater septemgeminus fons* [Here, O Father Thames, your seven sources]. Others say the real source is at Thames Head in a field near Tarlton, south-west of Cirencester, where there is a stone but no water, except in very wet winters. Take your pick. Today Father Thames reclines comfortably on the lockside at St John's Lock, Lechlade, which should not displease either camp. This figure was sculpted in the classical style by Rafaelle Monti from Portland cement and exhibited at the Great Exhibition of 1851. After surviving the Crystal Palace fire of 1936, it was bought by the Thames Conservancy and installed at Tarlton, but was later relocated due to vandalism.

Once on the run, the Thames is lauded and worshipped, both as Old Father Thames, as in Edmund Spenser's *The Faerie Queene* (1590): 'The noble Thamis, with all his goodly train', and as the goddess Isis:

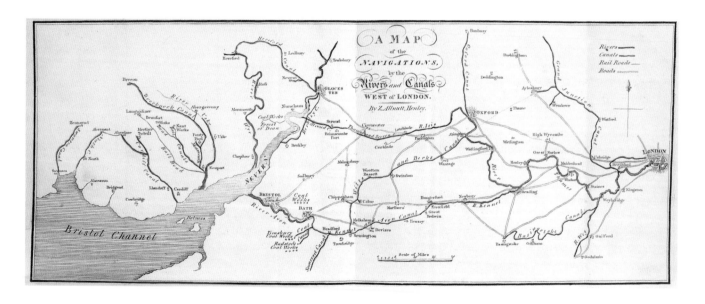

The Magna Carta Memorial
at Runnymede in Surrey,
supposedly where King John
and the Barons met to sign
the famous treaty in 1215.

Isis, whom British streams their monarch own…
And grateful light darts from his shining eyes
His grizzly beard all wet hangs dropping down
And gushing veins in wat'ry chanels run
The little fish in joyful numbers crowd
And silver swans fly o'er the crystal flood
And clap their snowy wings.

from *Marriage of Thame and Isis* by William Camden
(1586)

On early maps, such as John Speed's 1611 work, the Thames is identified as the Isis above its junction with the Thame. The latter was the old name for the whole river, with Isis a Roman creation that was reinvented by Camden and some Oxford dons from the sixteenth century onwards. Some say that Thame-Isis is the combination that spawned the final name, but this may be too neat and convenient an explanation. Today the Ordnance Survey labels the upper river as either Thames or Isis.

Like all rivers, the Thames absorbs and refocuses historical events, 'liquid history', as the writer John Burns would put it. One of the most important events in British history, and one of subsequent resonance for the rest of the world, took place on its banks on 15 June 1215: the signing of Magna Carta. The exact location of the signing of one of this country's most significant political, legal and social documents is actually rather uncertain. It is generally acknowledged to have been in a water meadow near Staines, now known as Runnymede and in the care of the National Trust, but some authorities have argued

The opening of Thomas Telford's St Katharine Dock on the Thames, 25 October 1828. Crowds of spectators watched the *Elizabeth* enter the basin.

that the event actually took place on a small island (or 'eyot') in the middle of the river, with others insisting that the ceremony occurred under the great yew tree at nearby Ankerwycke Nunnery. The document itself, a charter with 63 separate articles, was drafted in Latin by Stephen Langton, Archbishop of Canterbury, essentially as a peace treaty between the Crown and the power-hungry barons who had temporarily seized both London and King John. Yet it also established the principles of freedom guaranteed by law, and is the basis upon which we have been governed ever since.

Although the truce held for only two months before civil war broke out again, the Great Charter, as it was later called, was amended several times subsequently and finally reissued by Edward I as law in 1297. It served as a template for civil rights and social reform, and its provisions have been reinterpreted many times since, forming the basis of the Petition of Rights in 1628, of habeas corpus in 1679, of the American Constitution and even of the Constitution of independent India in 1947. Interestingly, the United States government tried to extract an original copy of Magna Carta in return for support of the British war effort, during their negotiations with the British in 1941 and before Pearl Harbour forced their hand.

Meanwhile, King John had met a watery fate. A year after Magna Carta, he died in Newark of dysentery contracted in the Fens. His treasures and baggage train were lost in the mist and swallowed up by quicksand as he attempted to cross the Wellstream near the Wash. Water was his undoing.

London was almost certainly a prehistoric crossing place, but it is uncertain precisely what sort of settlement may have existed on the banks of the river before the Romans arrived. Once they did, however, London soon developed as the hub of the new conquerors' British presence, their great roads of Ermine Street, the Fosse Way, the Icknield Way and Watling Street all converging here and crossing the Thames as fords. The first bridge, of wooden construction, was built c.AD50. Either side of it, a settlement and centre of supplies grew up rapidly, so that by the end of the first century AD there were some 30,000 souls living there. Among the Romans' most effective actions was the development of a riverside infrastructure of wharves and piers, which although repeatedly destroyed by various invaders, was always rebuilt. This enabled the Thames in London to develop and sustain a role as a real conduit of commerce and serve as the means by which the city was able to become the most important port in the world. The first stone bridge over the Thames was not built until 1176, on the site of the original Roman bridge, and it remained the only bridge – 'London' Bridge – in the city until 1749. Meanwhile, the river had become a true focal point, teeming with life and very much the centre of London. Peter Ackroyd, in *London: The Biography* (2000), highlights the symbiotic nature of the relationship between river and city:

> The city itself owes its character and appearance to the Thames. It was a place of 'crowded wharfs and people-pestered shores', the water continually in motion with 'shoals of labouring oars'. The movement and energy of London were the movement of horses and the energy of the river… Most Londoners earned their living directly off the river, or by means of the goods that were transported along it.

This 1872 depiction of a city warehouse by Gustave Doré gives a sense of the vast number of people employed on the Thames, as stevedores, boatmen, unloaders etc. Unloading cargo was a highly skilled and arduous task.

In addition to those who depended on the goods and products that either arrived in or left London via the Thames, the river itself sustained an entire community of people concerned solely with its administration and maintenance. These ranged from ferrymen to water bailiffs and pile-drivers. In 1598, there were an estimated 40,000 people earning a living on or about the river, the banks of which were swarming with activity, goods being loaded and unloaded, while the water churned around the hundreds of vessels, from skiffs to galleons, that were moored alongside. Although the river was very much a working place, with all the grime and hardship that this entailed, it was also used extensively for 'official' transportation and ceremonial purposes. Royal figures were regularly to be seen processing up and down in it, travelling to and from their palaces in extravagantly decorated and gilded barges. They included, in 1533, Henry VIII and his wife Anne Boleyn, accompanied by much pomp and circumstance, including 'trumpets, shawms, and other divers instruments, all the way playing and making great melody'. She was, of course, to take a much sadder river journey a few years later, through the Traitor's Gate at the Tower, to her execution.

Canaletto's *The Thames on Lord Mayor's Day, c.1747.* This celebrated work shows the scale and opulence of the Lord Mayor's party on the river. Water feasts on a grand scale.

The Thames was seen in its utmost grandeur on the occasion of the Lord Mayor's Show, which from the fifteenth century until 1856 took place on the river. All the city companies and guilds had barges, the more opulent among them covered in gold leaf and with silver oars, and upon which their members dined lavishly and ostentatiously. The whole spectacle must have seemed more akin to a Venetian carnival, a point which was surely not lost upon the artist Giovanni Canaletto, who visited London in the 1740s and whose extravagant (if rather idealised) views of the Thames and its waterfront remain powerful symbols of a river and city in the ascendant.

The role of the Thames as a focal point for endless activity did not cease when hard winters fell. When the river froze – which it did 23 times between 1620 and 1814 – it became the venue for frost fairs, among the most beguiling and atmospheric events of London's past, when the rumbustious character of the city spilled out onto the solid river. In 1564, Queen Elizabeth walked upon the ice in order to watch an archery contest, and in 1684 John Evelyn described a whole ox being roasted and printing presses being set up on the ice over the Thames. That particular occasion was called the 'blanket fair', because people erected tents made from their bedclothes on the ice. Charles II even hunted a fox on the river. Bowls were played, various races held, and coaches and sledges ran on the ice between Blackfriars and Westminster. Performing bears, bull baiting, itinerant musicians, hot potatoes and football, there was no end to the entertainment. Large-scale trade may have been at a standstill, but the ice was bedecked with stalls and stands selling all sorts of goods. Doubtless there was much profiteering, too, especially as certain commodities would have been in short supply due to the severe weather. The main reason for the build-up of ice was the constriction caused by the old London Bridge. Ice floes would jam between the narrow arches where there were watermills, which held the water back long enough for it to freeze. This bridge was replaced in 1831, and the Thames has not frozen over since.

The Fair on the Thames during the Great Frost of 1683–4. From an original drawing by Wyke in the British Museum, engraved by J. Stow in 1825.

Rivers and literature

Rivers have provided a constant source of inspiration to writers, and given us many intellectual and philosophical musings. Poets in particular value the language of the river, the lyrical dialogue between the water and the trees. One of the most remarkable literary figures associated with waterways is John Taylor, a self-educated wherryman and the so-called 'water poet'. Between 1618 and his poverty-stricken death in 1653, possibly from starvation, Taylor undertook twelve journeys across much of England, Wales and Scotland, often travelling by river and always writing up accounts of the places visited, and people met, en route. He published some two hundred works in total, ranging from pamphlets and religious tracts to a book of jokes and poems of his travels, which he modestly advertised as containing 'some passages of delightful mirth and recreation'. He also wrote a work on the superiority of river navigation over travel by land, and his lively and insightful descriptions are a fascinating snapshot of riverside life in Stuart Britain. In 1622, Taylor undertook an expedition from London to York, first sailing from the capital to Harwich, and continuing around the coast of East Anglia via various ports (including Cromer, where he was arrested as a pirate) to Boston in Lincolnshire, from where he travelled by inland waterways to Lincoln, Hull and finally York itself. The journey was often hardgoing:

> From thence [Lincoln] we past a ditch of weedes and mud,
> Which they doe (falsely) there call Forcedike Flood:

A solitary swan on the River Test near Stockbridge in Hampshire.

For I'l be sworne, no flood I could finde there,
But dirt and filth that scarce my boate would beare,
'Tis 8. miles long, and there our paines was such.
As all our travel did not seeme so much,
My men did wade, and drawe the boate like horses,
And scarce could tugge her on with all our forces:
Moyl'd, toyl'd, myr'd, tyr'd, still lab'ring, ever doing,
Yet were we 9. long houres that 8. miles going.

It was unusual for a writer to focus so closely on the hard practicalities of river transport. For most literary figures, especially those of the eighteenth and nineteenth centuries, rivers and waterways were the inspiration for romantic and aesthetic expression, or the context in which the artistic persona came to the fore most readily. The poet Shelley, for example, lived at Marlow in Buckinghamshire and in 1817 wrote most of his *Revolt of Islam* whilst recumbent in his boat, the *Vaga*, as it drifted on the Thames. The river environment was good for storytelling, too. Charles Dodgson, alias Lewis Carroll, first recounted the tale of *Alice's Adventures in Wonderland* to the Liddell family whilst on a boat journey from Oxford past Port Meadow to Godstow in 1862. William Morris, whose vast wealth came from a rich copper mine in the Tamar Valley, was another devotee of river travel. He lived at Kelmscott House in Hammersmith near the Thames from 1878 to 1896, and would travel from this to his rented property at Kelmscott Manor near Lechlade by boat. His *News from Nowhere* (1890) tells of such a journey.

Modern poets show a return, perhaps, to Taylor's more direct and realistic view of the trials, tribulations and threats that rivers can pose. Helen Dunmore, for example, sees the Thames as hungry:

Hungry Thames, I walk over the bridge
Half-scared you'll whittle me down

Where the brown water is eager
And tipped with foam

Hungry Thames (1997)

Craig Raine, meanwhile, reminds us that the river likes to flood:

Bright as Meringues the Swans sweep
Sideways down the passionate water

The boathouse punts are magnetised
And the rain scores a bull's eye every time

There is a bank of froth against the bridge
It has thrown in the sponge...

Floods (1979)

The fate of rivers smothered by industry and urban sprawl does not pass unnoticed. Roy Fisher's *Birmingham River* (1994) laments the disappearance of a primeval river overtaken by events:

Where's Birmingham River? Sunk.
Which river was it. Two. More or less.

History: we're on our tribal ground. When they
moved in from the Trent, the first English

entered the holdings and the bodies of people
who called the waters that kept them alive

Tame, the Dark River; these English spread their works
southward then westward, then all ways

Yet for many modern poets rivers remain enduringly positive and a raw expression of nature's power, constantly renewing and replenishing. Norman Nicholson's eulogy to one of the Lake District's most beautiful rivers focuses on both its natural abundance and its force:

Here from hazel islands in the late spring
The catkins fall and ride along the stream
Like little yellow weasels, and the soil is loosed
From bulbs of the white lily that smells of garlic
And dippers rock up and down on rubber legs
And long-tailed tits are flung through the air like darts;

To the River Duddon – Selected Poems, 1982

Chapter Five

❖

The canal age

PREVIOUS SPREAD Legging a canal
boat through the Butterley
Tunnel on the Cromford Canal
in Derbyshire, c.1900. The
tunnel was 3,000 yards long
and legging was a demanding
task. Men lay on their backs on
planks and walked the boat
through the tunnel while the
horse went over the top.

THE EVOLUTION OF BRITISH CANALS

One of the most exciting periods in the history of water landscapes was the shift from
river trade to transportation by canal. River conditions were unpredictable and
sometimes dangerous, whilst canals proved to be generally safe, reliable, direct and
constant. They were led overland into the hearts of towns, passing over hills and through
tunnels, connecting one river system to another and bringing sea trade further inland
than had been possible hitherto via rivers. This was truly a revolution in transport terms,
but the canal mania that spurred entrepreneurs and engineers into this dramatic and
Herculean activity was a long time in the making.

It was the Romans who first addressed the civil engineering problems later encountered
by the canal-builders. These were as much to do with drainage as with navigation. The
history of drainage has often been neglected in discussions of the evolution of canals, yet
many of the technical solutions used by the canal builders were pioneered much earlier
by drainage engineers. The Romans constructed aqueducts and other structures to draw
water from distant sources to towns and reservoirs.
These aqueducts later served as the means by which
canals could be carried over rivers and towns.
Techniques such as the puddling of channels with clay
(laying down a mixture of sand and clay, or 'puddle'
clay, to line the canal and make it watertight), the
building up of river banks and sea walls, piling, river
straightening, pumping and tunnelling, even the
construction of new rivers, were all drainage
techniques pioneered by the Romans and regularly
used in medieval times in locations such as the Fens of
eastern England, and the Somerset Levels and Moors.

Good canal-building, and good drainage, is all about
controlling and containing water, getting the levels
right and then leading it to the desired destination.
The Romans used large rivers like the Tiber to ship
grain up country to feed Rome, so when they came
to England in the first century AD, they set their
engineers the task of simplifying the river systems. In
Lincolnshire they constructed the Fossdyke, a water
link between Lincoln and the River Trent at Torksey.
After falling into disuse, it was scoured out again
during the reign of Henry I (1100–1135) and used
to ship the stone necessary for the construction of
Lincoln Cathedral. Grain was sent down the Trent and
then up the Ouse to York, to feed the garrison there.
It is still navigable today. The Romans also constructed
Car Dyke, a 6-foot-deep ditch from Lincoln to

An 1930s photograph of the
Fossdyke, which linked Lincoln
to the River Trent at Torksey.

Peterborough, joining the Cam and the Great Ouse. Car Dyke is an extraordinary landscape feature, which has recently been excavated at Helpringham Fen. At some points the ditch is clear, at others more difficult to trace – like much archaeology it has suffered from urban development and over-strenuous agriculture. Itchen Dyke, which ran between the south coast and Winchester, was another creation of Roman engineers. It was incorporated into the medieval Itchen river system and eventually into the Itchen Navigation, which was created formally by an Act of Parliament in 1665. Much of the navigation can still be seen today, though little remains of the Dyke itself.

The construction of such watery thoroughfares required widespread drainage and the cutting of integrated dykes. This in turn helped create extensive areas of fertile land suitable for agricultural use. The creation of productive land was a major objective of much of the drainage, particularly in areas where the abbeys and monasteries held sway. The thirteenth-century monk and historian William of Malmesbury wrote of his regard for the Benedictine monks of Thorney in Cambridgeshire who had drained much of the land around their abbey and 'created a paradise' for crops of many kinds, including vines.

Early canals and new rivers

The oldest post-Roman canal in England was started in 1563, on the tidal section of the River Exe in Devon. An adaptation of the river, it led from opposite Topsham up to Exeter, an important cathedral city with a healthy woollen cloth trade. The only serious problem en route was a weir that had been constructed in the thirteenth century by Isabella, Countess of Devon (the weir's name was later changed to Countess Wear to reflect the countess's endeavours). The weir helped to power the local watermills but had also been built as a deliberate obstruction, to prevent vessels from going up to Exeter. The countess's family, the Courtenays, controlled the port of Topsham and had a monopoly on the haulage to Exeter. A running battle, both legal and physical, went on for over 300 hundred years and ended only when Henry Courtenay was executed for treason in 1539. The good burghers of Exeter seized their chance and were given royal assent to carry out essential repairs to the Exe, including new diggings and the

plucke downe, digge, moyne, breke, banke and caste upp all and all manner of weyres rockes, sandes, gravell, and other lettes and noysaunces whatsoever they be in the saide river... and make all other thinges requisite and necesssarie wherby the saide shippes, boates and vessels may have their sure course and recourse in the saide River to & from youre saide Cittie.

from *An Act concerning the amending of the River and Port of Exeter*, 1539.

This was an expensive enterprise and required some hefty fundraising before work could actually start. Eventually, in 1563, John Trew of Glamorganshire was hired for the sum of £225 and a percentage of the subsequent tolls to

…conduct and make the Haven of the Citie in suche sorte as boates and vessels laden with Tenne Tonnes vightes at the least shall at all tydes & tydes passe & repasse to & from the seas unto the Cities walls.

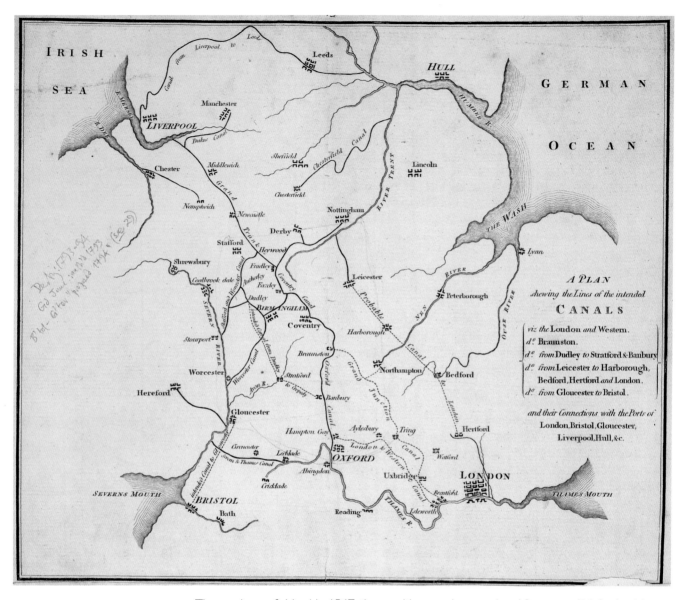

This 1792 map of the lines of intended canals in England shows very clearly the beginnings of the canal age and how important it was to link north with south-east and west.

The work was finished in 1567, the resulting canal measuring 4.9 metres (16 feet) wide and 90 centimetres (3 feet) deep. It had three pairs of lock gates, the upper set of these having what we know of today as 'mitred gates', with paddles to let the water in. There were pools 30.5 metres (100 feet) long, which served as passing spaces through which gangs of lighters could pass easily in both directions. The system was fed by water drawn from the Exe's higher reaches. Exeter certainly benefited from the canal but, as with all canals, the sums needed for maintenance and dredging were a constant burden. It fell into disrepair during the civil war, but was rebuilt in 1698–9 and widened to 13 metres (42 feet), with a depth of 4 metres (14 feet). During this time it boomed, from the trade in serge cloth.

Meanwhile, in eastern England in the seventeenth century, work was under way to assist with the drainage of the Fens, through a system of improvements and the creation of 'new rivers'. Efforts had already been made in the second half of the 1500s to control flooding by the construction of wind engines (proto-windmills with water scoops attached) and 'Courts of Sewers' had, as in other parts of England, been responsible for maintaining waterways through bank consolidation and periodic scouring, designed to remove silt and blockages. Silting was a major problem, and began to have a serious impact on inland ports such as Littleport on the Bedford Levels near Ely, which became increasingly inaccessible to boats of any great size.

In the early seventeenth century, foreign drainage engineers like Cornelius Vermuyden were brought in to apply the latest Dutch drainage techniques to these problems. The main mover behind this scheme was the Earl of Bedford, who with his fellow fourteen 'gentlemen adventurers' put up the prodigious funds required for the enormous programme of works to go ahead. The objective was to drain the marshland, contain the ravages of winter flooding and create proper thoroughfares of water through which the region's main towns – including Bedford – could be connected to the sea. A 21-mile drain – the Old Bedford River – was cut in a straight line from Earith to Denver, to take

water from the River Ouse out towards King's Lynn and the Wash. A second river, the New Bedford or Hundred Foot, was cut parallel to it and embanked, the area between being designed to serve as a safety valve in times of flood. A rash of new windmills was erected and used to pump water off the marshland and into the newly cut rivers and canals via a network of sluices and drains. The idea was to bring marginal wetland into profitable agricultural production, at least for those who had purloined this new land; Parliament had sanctioned the allocation of 35.5 hectares (95,000 acres) of fen, which had served as de facto common land to those who lived there, as recompense to the scheme's investors. Not surprisingly, there was considerable opposition from local people, many of whom, being wildfowlers or fishermen, relied on the traditional fen environment for their livelihood.

Yet there was something inexorable about the march of the new rivers and 'navigations'. The vision of those behind such schemes soon became unstoppable,

Narrowboat tranquillity. Second homes moored on the River Wey Navigation in Surrey.

and entrepreneurial imaginations were constantly seeking to connect navigable rivers with large towns and even the coast. One such enterprise was the River Wey Navigation in Surrey, which connected Guildford with the Thames at Weybridge and is considered to be the finest work of its kind undertaken in the seventeenth century. The river has a fall of 26 metres (86 feet) between Guildford wharf and the Thames, a size of drop not encountered in the Fens. Devised by Sir Richard Weston (1591–1652), the navigation contains ten pound locks, four weirs, twelve 'new' bridges (ie built as part of the scheme). Seven out of the fifteen miles of river were artificially cut. The Wey Navigation opened in 1653 and its instigator was much acclaimed; Edmund Gibson, the ecclesiastic and writer, had this to say about Sir Richard in 1695:

> The River Wye [sic] which the Thames receives, brings in great profits to that part of the county, being navigable by the industry of that worthy Knight Sir Richard Weston of Sutton place; to whom the whole shire is obliged as for this, so, for several other improvements, particularly clover and Sainefoine.

> from *Britannia* by William Camden (1795 edition)

Eighty years later the Wey Navigation was extended to Godalming, and in the 1820s it was connected to the River Arun by the Wey and Arun canal, which provided a navigable connection between the Thames and Portsmouth. It became an important means of trade and despite being rendered increasingly redundant by the coming of the railways, was still being used commercially until 1960 or so. Today much of it is owned by the National Trust, and a visitor centre at Dapdune Wharf in Guildford explains the history of the navigations and the people who once worked along it. One of the last great Wey barges is also moored there.

Locks and controls

Water in the new rivers and navigations was increasingly controlled by the construction and manipulation of locks. The use of locks goes back over two thousand years and prior to the invention of the double lock, 'flash' locks were the most common device, particularly around weirs. Flash locks were single gates, usually built into a dam constructed to raise the water level of a river for navigational purposes. The gate could then be lifted and boats either let down or winched up. The procedure for a boat travelling downstream was straightforward enough, insofar as the gate was lifted and the boat would shoot through, often at some speed. For boats travelling upstream an altogether more perilous action was required, whereby the boat was connected to a winch or a team of horses, the gate opened, and the boat then drawn through the opening against the powerful current. Accidents were not uncommon.

The first flash lock recorded on the Thames was at Marlow in 1306 and by Elizabethan times there were 70 of them in the country. Flash locks were replaced increasingly by double locks as the only economic way of changing level, and the last Thames flash lock in use was at Eynsham in 1930. The far more efficient double lock consisted of two mitred gates at either end of the lock, with internal sluices and paddles, so enabling the boat to rapidly either rise or fall to gain a new level.

The whole lock system – and the control it gave over the passage of goods and people along the canals – led to no end of strife. Disputes were common between millers and bargees, as the miller often controlled the lock beside the weir and would hold up river traffic while he ground his morning's corn. Equally, if a miller released his water at the wrong time it could cause serious problems further downstream. Some millers would hold boats and barges to ransom, a situation that did not please architect Sir Christopher Wren when he was trying to ship stone from Taynton in Gloucestershire to his new London cathedral of St Paul's. Wren recommended that the statutory bodies called 'Commissions of Sewers' be encouraged to take more interest in their work. Many major rivers had commissions ostensibly in charge of their maintenance, but in reality their performance was patchy. Even in cases where a commissioner was proactive in managing and developing the river in his charge, there was much opposition from road carriers, who felt their interests to be under threat. Violence was not uncommon. Navigation works at Waltham on the River Lea in Essex were destroyed in 1592, and between 1718 and 1723, when canal-builder John Hore was building the River Kennet Navigation from Reading to Newbury, his workers were molested regularly by mill owners and gangs sent out by the mayor and recorder of Reading to break down the locks. As a result of such disputes, calls increased for greater statutory control and regulation of rivers and canals.

The golden age of canals

The construction of the Newry Canal in Northern Ireland during the 1730s marked the beginning of the heyday of British canals. The first canal to go over the summit of a hill, it

provided a vital link between landlocked Lough Neagh and the port of Newry, as well as to the developing collieries in the area, which were struggling to reach their potential markets. The suggestion of constructing a navigation between Lough Neagh and the sea had been made as early as the 1670s, but it was not until 1703 that a proper survey was carried out, and only in 1731 did work begin. The canal was completed early in 1742 and in spring that year the first cargo of Tyrone coal sailed into Dublin. The canal crossed 18 miles of rough country and rose to a height of 24 metres (78 feet) above sea level. It was here that the first incline plains in the British Isles were constructed in 1777, the work of a German engineer called Richard Cassels. These were extraordinary devices for raising canal barges in long tanks of water, with a water-fed, counter-balanced gravity system.

A 1868 map of Ireland showing the river catchment areas and Lough Neagh. It was here that early advances in canal engineering were pioneered.

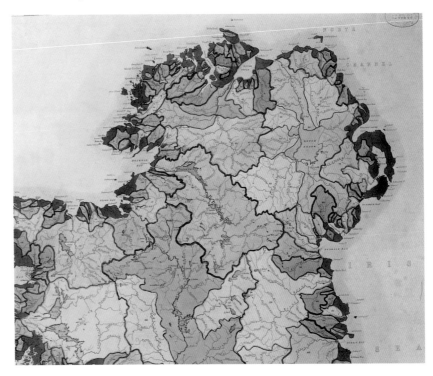

James Brindley, 1716–1772, was one of the great pioneer canal-builders. He was born near Buxton and started life as an apprentice millwright. In the background can be seen the Barton Aqueduct, one of the wonders of the age, which allowed ships to sail over the River Irwell.

Coal was also a motivating factor in the construction of the St Helen's Canal, which made the Sankey brook navigable down to the Mersey. It was designed to bypass the turnpikes that were making coal prohibitively expensive in Liverpool, and opened in 1757. A few years later, in 1763, the famous Bridgewater Canal was built near Manchester to link the Duke of Bridgewater's coalmines in Worsley to the city some 10 miles away. Hitherto, the coal had been transported by packhorse, over poorly maintained and time-consuming roads. The impact this had on the price of the coal was central to the argument the Duke made when petitioning Parliament for the necessary Act to allow him to cut the canal – it would enable him to get his coal more quickly and more cheaply to Manchester, thereby benefiting his customers. The Act was passed, the first of its kind, and in 1761 the canal was opened. One of its most extraordinary features was the stone-built aqueduct by which the canal passed over the River Irwell; an amazing sight for its time. The way in which the Bridgewater Canal came about was typical of many new canals, the result of an individual, or group of like-minded souls, possessing the commercial clout and vision to initiate hugely ambitious projects. These were often anything but straightforward, not simply in engineering terms, but also from the point of view of securing the necessary Parliamentary approval and obtaining the agreement of landowners, through whose land the proposed canals would cut.

In the rough-and-tumble of the canal-building age, some outstanding characters emerged. One such figure was the former millwright and then surveyor James Brindley, who, after his involvement with the Bridgewater Canal, compiled plans for numerous other canal schemes, but who died in 1772 before many of his projects could come to fruition. His great vision was that of the Grand Cross, an ambitious scheme by which canals would connect the Mersey to the Thames and the Trent to the Severn. The first part of this project was achieved, with the help of Josiah Wedgwood, and consisted of the Trent and Mersey canal of 'Grand Trunk', completed in 1777. Wedgwood built his famous factory at Etruria, and the canal allowed him both to import Cornish clay for processing in his factories and transport his celebrated pottery to markets across the country – with a much reduced chance of breakage than would have been the case by road. The route involved the construction of a tunnel at Harecastle extending to a mile and a half in length; canal barges had to be 'legged' through the tunnel by men lying flat on their backs, their boots on the walls so they could 'walk' the boat forward. Legging continued long after steam tugs had been invented, particularly for dangerous cargoes like explosives. Indeed, gunpowder factories were sometimes specially positioned near canals precisely so the powder could be transported safely without endangering the general public. Another great figure of the canal age was Thomas Telford (1757–1834). A shepherd's son born in Eskdale in Cumberland, Telford was apprenticed to a stonemason in Langholm, and later went to London, where he worked as a journeyman mason on Somerset House. Further advancement depended on patronage, and he was lucky to be taken under the wing of William Pulteney, who secured him a job as surveyor for Shropshire, where he worked on both the Shrewsbury and Ellesmere canals. It was Telford's idea to use iron for aqueducts, the most famous of which is the Pontcysyllte on the Chirk and Llangollen Canal. Bridges were also his forte, and he later built both the Menai and the Conway. In 1818, he became the first President of the Institute of Civil Engineers, no mean feat for a shepherd's son. Not many engineers have a new town named after them, either.

Sir Edward Leader Williams (1828–1910) was the chief engineer of the Severn navigation and then the Weaver navigation. It was his idea to construct the ingenious Anderton Boat Lift (designed by Edwin Clark), an extraordinary structure labelled 'the cathedral of the canals' and designed to speed up the movement of cargo between the Trent and Mersey Canal and the River Weaver. The first of its type in the world, the lift consisted of two vast water-filled chambers, or caissons, which counterbalanced

each other, taking boats up and down between river and canal, a difference in height of some 15 metres (50 feet). The lift took three years to build and opened in 1875. After falling into disrepair in the early 1980s, it was subsequently restored and officially reopened to traffic in 2002.

The generally piecemeal approach to canal-building, whereby individuals pursued their own favourite projects, often tied to particular functions or objectives, or wealthy client's whims, led to a sometimes uneven and incoherent national network. For example, not all canals were built to the same width or depth, thereby restricting the type of craft that could use them. Such inconsistencies were not helpful, and this was especially the case with the network of canals built by different companies in central England between

The Anderton Boat Lift, which connects the Trent and Mersey Canal to the River Weaver (with a difference in level of 15 metres/50 feet) is a legend in its own lifetime. This extraordinary structure was built in 1875 and is now fully restored. The lift is operated by a series of water-filled caissons that act as counterbalances.

The excavation of the Manchester Ship Canal: Eastham Cutting, with Mount Manisty in the distance by Benjamin Williams Leader (1831–1923). The canal was a brave but ultimately very expensive project to make Manchester an inland port in its own right.

London and Birmingham during the period 1790 to 1929. The companies eventually amalgamated, making it possible to create a 'union' of canals which could form a continuous link between Birmingham, London and other important industrial areas, such as Leicester. So the Grand Union Canal was born. Running for 137 miles from the Thames at Brentford into the heart of Birmingham (a separate spur breaks off at Braunston in Northamptonshire and leads to Leicester), the canal has over 160 locks. Regular boatmen would claim to be able to do the 137-mile journey in five days.

One of the oddest canals ever built was the Royal Military Canal on Romney Marsh in Kent. This was constructed between 1804 and 1807 as a defensive canal during the Napoleonic Wars, the intention being to create not only an obstacle to invasion but also a means of moving local troops around should the French force ever land on English soil. Sixty-two feet wide and nine feet deep, the Royal Military Canal was dug by 1,000 soldiers and stretches from Iden Lock and the River Rother to West Hythe Sluice, a distance of 19 miles. It was later extended in the east to Shornecliffe and in the west using the rivers Rother, Tillingham and Brede; it thence reaches out to Pett Level beyond Winchelsea. A middle section between Warehorne and Appledore is cared for by the National Trust. After the Napoleonic period the canal served as a commercial waterway between Hythe and Rye until 1909, and when invasion loomed again in 1940 it was kitted out with pillboxes, several of which remain today. Now it serves as a peaceful waterway with much wildlife interest, and as a haunt of fishermen.

Although the heyday of canal-building was from 1750–1850, when over 4,000 miles of canals were constructed across Britain, one of the most important canals – the Manchester Ship Canal – was not completed until the 1890s. The objective was to give Manchester direct access to the sea, thereby avoiding the expensive road and rail options that operated via Liverpool, which was accused by Mancunian businessmen and consumers of holding landlocked Manchester to ransom with its high tolls and tariffs. Oldham traders were quoted as saying that it was cheaper to send their goods the 100 miles by road to the port of Hull on the east coast than to transport them the 35 miles to Liverpool and have to pay exorbitant harbour dues and levies. The concept of the canal was a source of great civic pride, and much celebration followed Parliament's final agreement to the plan. Work commenced in 1887 and the canal was opened with considerable fanfare in 1894. It was connected to the River Mersey at Port Sunlight, where the Lever brothers' factory was soon exporting some 1,600 tons of Sunlight soap a week through the Ship Canal. The canal certainly boosted Manchester's trading status, especially her exports, and many engineering feats had been achieved en route, including the construction of the massive 1450-ton Barton Swing Aqueduct (which allowed the Bridgewater Canal to pass over the Manchester Ship Canal, so replacing the earlier eighteenth-century aqueduct), and the Swing Road Bridge at Salford Quays. However impressive these achievements may have been, financially the canal was a disaster. The works went way over budget, with the total bill coming to more than £15 million (£980 million in today's terms), of which £1 million alone went on the 16,000 navvies' wages. Several of its investors went bankrupt as a result.

Engineers, navvies and canal people

Canals and their construction were very much at the cutting edge of civil engineering. The roles of chief engineer, resident engineer and contractor slowly evolved out of necessity, the country never having seen engineering works on such a large scale before. The chief engineer was responsible for drawing up the plans and seeing the scheme through Parliament, whilst the resident engineer coped with the day-to-day physical problems of the construction, as well as with ordering and inspecting the work and placating awkward landowners. He also dealt with the contractors, who in turn controlled the rough-and-ready armies of strong but heavy-drinking navvies or 'navigators'. Yet these navvies are the unsung heroes of the canal age, for with their picks, spades and wheelbarrows they reshaped Britain's waterways.

It is estimated that in the 1790s there were over 50,000 navvies working on Britain's canals. They often came from poor rural communities, not just in England but also from Ireland and Scotland, and many were former agricultural workers, forced to leave the land due to lack of work or poor pay. For many of them, working on the canals became a way of life and they never returned home. Navvies accomplished extraordinary feats with the limited tools at their disposal; a good man could shift 12 cubic yards of earth a

Navvies hard at work on the Manchester Ship Canal. The sheer physical labour required to dig the canals cannot be over-emphasised.

day. Their pay varied considerably. In the 1770s men working on the Oxford Canal were paid about 1s 3d a day, but twenty years later navvies on the Lancaster Canal were being paid 2s 6d a day. Agricultural wages were little more than 7s a week, so canal work was very well paid by the standards of the time.

Navvies received a generally bad press, but many reports were biased. Unruly behaviour was the norm across the country in the late eighteenth and early nineteenth centuries, with bread riots and machine riots commonplace. The Industrial Revolution was not unduly concerned with issues such as health and safety, a fair working wage or human rights. An increasingly frustrated and undernourished workforce felt the need to give vent to its feelings. In *The History of Railways connecting London and Birmingham* (1839) Peter Lecount described navvies as 'the Terror of the surrounding country; they are as completely a class by themselves as Gypsies. Possessed of all the daring recklessness of the smuggler, without any of his redeeming qualities, their ferocious behaviour can only be equalled by the brutality of their language.'

Navvies were often paid with tokens that could only be redeemed at certain shops or pubs. In 1810 navvies who had been working on the Grand Western Canal between Wellington and Tiverton had difficulty in getting paid, due to a shortage of available change. In a drunken rage many of them descended on the village of Sampford Peverell. A rumpus ensued, with one navvie shot dead, another badly wounded and several villagers badly beaten up.

However, a report from Berwick-on-Tweed in 1846 casts a very different light on the navies there:

> Their conduct has exceeded in decorum what had been previously expected. Certainly there were drunken brawls, but beyond these they had not rendered themselves obnoxious in any way to the community. One thing is certain, that never were person and property in the borough more free from attack than they have been in the last eighteen months…

Of course, engineers and navvies were only part of the canal workforce. Carpenters, pile-drivers, puddlers, gate men, sawyers, pitmen, stonemasons, bricklayers and carters were all essential to the smooth completion of a project. Once the construction of a canal was finished, a new group of people moved in to start earning a living from the opportunities the new waterway provided, as lock-keepers, labour for loading/unloading, or as vendors of goods and services required by bargees. These canal communities were close-knit affairs, many with their own distinctive families of boat gypsies, 'the people of

A navvies' village at Acton Grange near Warrington, c.1890. Villages such as this sprung up overnight to meet the accommodation needs of the Ship Canal workers.

Canal boat men and women were very proud of their skills and way of life, dressing the part and decorating their boats with bright colours. Women raised children 'on the cut' and educated them as they went.

the cut', very proud and very competent. Women handled boats as well as men and whole families lived aboard, accommodated in small back cabins heated by pot-bellied wood-burning stoves. It was a nomadic existence, but they made the most of their cramped surroundings and decorated their floating homes with narrowboat paintings – vivid stylised pictures of subjects such as castles and horses – as well as roses and lace. Canal communities flourished in places like Stourport (Worcestershire), Shardlow (Derbyshire), Sharpness (Gloucestershire), Ellesmere Port (Cheshire) and Gas Street Basin in Birmingham. Canals became an essential part of any working town, the towpaths serving as convenient walkways. Hitching a ride on the fly boats that worked through the night even became a cheap and convenient way of getting from one town to another.

The decline of the canals

Although some canal projects came to nothing or ended in financial ruin, most proved a great success. Britain's canal network played a central role in the Industrial Revolution and made possible the cheap and reliable transportation of a huge range of goods to many parts of the country. The landscape was transformed, both physically and psychologically, as regions were put into contact with each other in a way that would have been inconceivable a few decades earlier, and goods became much more widely distributed than ever before.

Sadly, only 100 years into the canal age, the railway appeared, signalling the beginning of a long decline for canals. Canal transportation suddenly seemed slow and outdated. Despite this, many canals did work well into the twentieth century, some even enjoying a brief resurgence during the Second World War, for example when women were brought in to help keep cargo moving on the Grand Union. Some of the last cargoes to be carried by canal were moved during the 1960s: milk for the Bournville chocolate factory in Birmingham, coal from Ashby de la Zouch down the Grand Union to Camden Basin, and the Rose's lime juice run from London Docks.

Many canals fell into disrepair. Some small ones, like the Tavistock Canal and Mary Tavy in Devon, were adapted to provide hydroelectric power, but most were finally eclipsed by the motorways. During the great winter freeze of 1962–3 many haulage contracts went out to lorries and never returned to the canals. A number of industrial cities had already let their canals become derelict by then. The industry that fed them collapsed, the canals deteriorating into a sad sight and a byword for urban deprivation. They became dumping grounds for supermarket trolleys, toxic chemicals, plastic bags, rubbish and even cars.

However, the decline of the canals did have some unexpected benefits. Some became havens for wildlife, their banks overgrown, their water plants and creatures left undisturbed. Canals provided corridors of wetland habitat through areas that were nowhere near existing rivers, and as enclosures and drainage gobbled up wetland, canals became thin winding threads of refuge through an increasingly intensive prairie of agriculture. As they dropped out of commercial usage, so their value to wildlife increased. Today canals provide a vital lifeline for many species, especially in urban areas, and particularly since pollution levels have been reduced in recent years. For example, the Rochdale Canal is now home to extensive colonies of common water-plantain, scarce-fringed water lily and water soldier, and there are stands of water violet in many of the canals around Greater Manchester.

Forty years after what seemed to be the death knell of Britain's canals, a renaissance is taking place. Canals are experiencing a major revival, with many under restoration and ambitious schemes to rehabilitate others (see Chapter Eight). Twenty-first century leisure demands have taken over from the hard graft of two centuries ago, and now we are encouraged as consumers to use our canals once again. These are exciting times along the canal, and a fitting vindication of the blood, sweat and tears expended by the thousands that planned, plotted and toiled away in one of the great infrastructural projects in British history.

The common water-plantain can serve as a barometer of waterway health, soon disappearing from polluted rivers and canals.

Chapter Six

❖

River nature

TREES ALONG THE BANK

The alder is one of the commonest waterside trees and dependent on damp conditions.

Water is the source of life, and so it is no surprise that waterside habitats provide some of the richest environments for wildlife. Indeed, certain freshwater wetlands can support more species of plant, animal and bird than any other habitat. Paradoxically, others can be virtually sterile, usually because of high acidity levels in the local soil or water. Whatever their intrinsic characteristics, one thing all waterways have in common is that they are vulnerable to disturbance and pollution. During the first half of the twentieth century, many of them were totally destroyed, sacrificed to development or agricultural improvement, a process that saw water meadows drained, riverside trees torn out, banks buried under concrete, vegetation scoured out and the water itself brutalised into a tame channel running in a straight line. Only in more recent decades has the tide of destruction receded, and not a moment too soon. Some species were driven almost to the brink of extinction, and now millions of pounds are being spent restoring and protecting the habitats they require.

Visually, waterside trees are intensely appealing. Who can fail to be charmed by the sight and sound of riverside trees reflected in the water and rustling in the breeze? Yet the role of trees along our waterways is far more than merely an aesthetic one. They constitute a valuable home for wildlife, not only in their own right but also via the diverse habitats created through the shade and dappled light they provide. Their roots also stabilise banks, and their leaves help create invertebrate-rich silt on riverbeds. Although most trees do not enjoy the constant close proximity of water, several species are able to survive both periodic flooding and permanently wet conditions. These

PREVIOUS SPREAD **Dovedale at Ravens Tor. The River Dove is one of England's last remaining strongholds for the native white-clawed crayfish.**

include the alder, one of the most ubiquitous of waterside trees. Alder belongs to the same family as birch, and in spring the male tree carries bunches of red catkins. The traditional name of alder is aller and this is often reflected in place names, such as Aller in Somerset, Northallerton in Yorkshire and Aldershot in Surrey.

In *Sylva* (1664), John Evelyn had this to say about the alder:

> The alder is of all other, the most faithful lover of water and boggy places… Of old they made boats of the greater parts of this tree… And as then, so now, are overgrown Alders frequently sought after for such buildings as lye continually under water, where it will harden like a very stone.

So hard and water-resistant is alder wood that it was used to make clogs. It was also the favoured wood for building wharves and jetties, and is still used for stabilising the banks of rivers and lakes. The use of alder charcoal for gunpowder was once widespread, and as many gunpowder mills were water-powered, this made perfect sense. In many localities alders were a managed resource, subject to coppicing (to which it responds very well, shooting from the stump) or pollarding every three or four years. The wood was not the only product; the bark is useful for tanning, and gives a strong black dye when combined with iron sulphate. Alder carr – thickets of alder growing in saturated conditions – is a very valuable habitat, particularly for the willow tit, one of Britain's most rapidly declining birds. In autumn and winter alders are excellent places to look for seed-eating species such as goldfinch, redpoll and siskin.

Other regular sights along British waterways are various varieties of willow and poplar. The list of different willow species is long, but white willow and crack willow are common natives. Both grow quite tall, and despite often splitting and collapsing, branches and stems will continue to grow and even root on contact with the ground. Regular pollarding can help to keep the tree healthy, whilst the opening up of cavities can provide excellent habitats for owls and roosting bats. Also widespread – and more well known – are the sallows, members of the willow family and notable for their fluffy golden catkins, the famous 'pussy willow'. There are three native species of sallow, all of which grow well in waterlogged soil.

Willows are best known as the source for 'withies', thin poles that are used for a number of purposes. The poles are the

White willow can be distinguished by the faintly silvery appearance of its bark and leaves.

Sallow, also known as goat willow or pussy willow, grows enthusiastically in many waterside situations and is a valuable habitat for small birds and insects.

The arrowhead is usually found in slow-moving rivers, canals and ditches.

stems of the willow, either cut from pollarded trees or coppiced from the stool at ground level. Depending on the length and width of the stem, they have been used traditionally as the sails in a hurdle, ridge poles in thatching, hop poles, vine supports, beehives, crab pots, shoemaker's lasts, trugs, plates and even the bottoms of carts. The young and supple stems of osier willows were notable for use in basket-making, and they are still grown commercially in 'withy beds'.

One particularly interesting willow hybrid is now known as bat willow, famous as the source of wood for cricket bats. Harvested every twenty years, this variety is often grown in East Anglia and Somerset. It reaches prodigious heights. One famous specimen, felled in 1888, grew to over 30.5 metres (100 feet) and yielded 1,179 cricket bats. Equally celebrated, and closely associated with water, the highly ornamental weeping willow was imported into Britain from China in 1701 by a surgeon in the East India Company called James Cunningham, and became very fashionable later that century, when chinoiserie was all the rage. Today it is seen as often on willow pattern plates as it is in parks and gardens.

Other water-loving trees include the rare and very tall black poplar, which can reach 36.5 metres (120 feet), white poplar, Lombardy poplar and the aspen, which quivers and rustles like the silver birch and is known perhaps unfairly as 'old wives' tongues'. The noise made by the foliage is very similar to that of water and often confused with it.

Waterside flora

The profusion of plants around water in summer can be quite staggering. Not only is the number of species quite considerable, but their sheer abundance can sometimes mean that the water itself almost disappears from sight. In the maelstrom of vegetation it can be difficult to remember that each species will have slightly different requirements from its neighbour, and that many are sensitive to the slightest change in local conditions, and particularly to changing water levels. Generally speaking, waterside plants can be divided into two groups: those that thrive in, or on, the open water; and those whose preference is for the marginal habitats, where they can keep their roots moist and most of their foliage dry.

Water lilies belong firmly to the first group, and are among our most beautiful plants. Four species are native to Britain, although many other varieties can be found living in the wild, naturalised escapees from gardens and parks. All water lilies require slow-moving water, and most anchor their roots in the silt and mud on the bottom of the river or lake. Their large leaves float on the surface and the flower stems push up from below towards the light. Three of the four native species have yellow flowers, and two are relatively common, found widely in rivers, lakes and canals. The white water lily is less well distributed, but can be found more frequently in lakes at high altitudes. Meanwhile, water lilies have long attracted the attentions of artists and literary folk. On the River Stour in Dorset, the dialect word for the yellow water lily is 'clote', as demonstrated in this line by the nineteenth-century poet, William Barnes: 'the flow'r afloat, the golden zummer clote'.

Although most plants are tied to a particular habitat, others are more flexible – none more so than members of the water-crowfoot family. These plants change their structure depending on the depth of the water, and several distinct species have evolved to fill each niche. In shallow streams, ivy-leaved and round-leaved crowfoots prevail, whilst in the deeper rivers one finds the brook, common, fan-leaved, pond, river, stream (misnamed, given its habitat preference!) and thread-leaved varieties, each one preferring slightly different conditions. Although there is some overlap in certain locations, it is highly unusual to find more than three species of water crowfoot growing in the same stretch of water. All thrive in open water, away from the banks, and the fan-leaved water crowfoot can even flower underwater, via the creation of its own air bubble.

The exotic pink blooms of the amphibious bistort are a common sight along many waterways in summer.

Another example of a plant that has evolved separate forms to cope with different environments is the amphibious bistort. A shorter variety of this species can be found in dry conditions and can be a common weed in fields, whereas a taller form inhabits ditches and canals, the pink flowerheads standing high above floating, oblong-shaped leaves. It grows in much the same aquatic environment as the scarce arrowhead, a member of the plantain family noted for its distinctive arrow-shaped leaves. Common water-plantain is the most widespread member of the plantain genus, although it has declined markedly in some areas as a result of pollution. Its particular niche is mud, in which it thrives.

The reed warbler is a summer migrant to Britain and common in beds of *Phragmites*. It weaves a basket-shaped nest between the stems, and frequently plays host to the parasitic cuckoo.

Most other plantlife hugs the shore. Among the taller members of the bankside community are the rushes, sedges and grasses, which can be found in abundance along most waterways. Foremost in height terms is the common reed, or *Phragmites*, which despite tending to follow the contours of the shore, does require its roots and lower reaches to be waterlogged. When conditions are right the species forms dense stands, of huge importance to particular species of bird, most notably the bittern, as well as small passerines such as the sedge warbler, reed warbler and bearded tit. The latter species is drawn to *Phragmites* by its seedheads, the autumn product of the delightful summer 'plumes', which

ABOVE In late summer the characteristic heads of the bulrush burst open and the seeds within are distributed by wind action.

BELOW Nowadays wild water-cress is often contaminated by liver-fluke, and should be cooked before eating.

help make this plant one of the great summer sights of our waterways. Its beauty is matched by its practicality, as common reed was traditionally one of the most important waterway products. Used for a range of purposes but most notably thatching, it was once harvested in enormous quantities, particularly in East Anglia and on the Somerset Levels and Moors. Norfolk reed was the most valued, but in recent years has been dramatically undercut by cheaper (and to many minds, inferior quality) East European imports. However, with reed cutting now a vital component in wetland management, British reed is making a comeback.

Other types of grass, rush and sedge were put to practical purpose by those living and working along the waterways. Soft-rush was one of the most widely used; the pith was stripped out of its long thin stems and served as a taper or wick. These 'rushlights', popular for their clear and smokeless flame, remained the main source of domestic lighting in more modest waterside dwellings until well into the twentieth century. When dipped in wax, the velvety spikes of the majestic reed mace or bulrush, packed with fluffy seed, also burn well and were often used as torches. Equally, the stems of the larger species of rush, as well as plants such as giant hogweed, were stuffed with tow or waste flax soaked in tallow. These also served as lights during the hours of darkness and were used by fishermen (who called them 'keckies') to mark landing stages on foggy nights. Cut by hand and sickle, rushes served as thatching material and, like reed, were used as the upholstery in rustic chairs and stools, made into mats, and used as bedding, as well as being the most common sort of floor covering in many country cottages.

Water-cress is arguably the most commercial waterside plant. A native species which favours fast-flowing streams, especially those on chalky soils, it was long picked and eaten by local people. However, during the nineteenth century it became more widely popular (partly in response to the publicity surrounding its medicinal qualities) and commercial nurseries were established, the cress grown in special beds fed by natural streams or boreholes. Hampshire, Wiltshire, Dorset and the Chilterns were all notable cress-growing areas, with much of the produce being taken to London for sale. Parts of Lincolnshire were also famous for cress, as shown in the photograph opposite. John Stennett of Bourne worked on the town's cressbeds in the 1950s:

In the period of my employ, we used water from artesian wells that had been specially sunk by the firm and this was diverted through the concrete-sided beds as a continuous running stream day and night. It was pure water of a high quality, clean and palatable, and we always filled our kettle with it to make the tea. Throughout the year, we had to grow the watercress plants, fertilise them and use large water, a tried and tested system of splitting them and forcing them to multiply and so increase production. These rakes were about 4 feet wide with 9-inch pegs or teeth and were quite heavy for a young lad, especially when using one all day. We spent most of our time outdoors, apart from short breaks in the shed, and we wore rubber waders for most of the day and stood on wooden planks that stretched over the plants across the width of each bed. The depth of water was about 18 inches.

In the springtime, the plants would flower and spread to a great thickness and shortly after flowering would come the cutting season. Cress was cut using long bladed knives and collected into bunches and we gauged a bunch size by using the thumb and forefinger and then secured them with rubber bands. We used to hold four bunches in the gaps between our fingers and thumb in either hand and then chop off the straggly stems at the end with a downward movement of the knife near the knuckle joints. When gathered, the cress was transported into a cleaning and preparing shed with flat wooden wheelbarrows. Ladies were employed during the harvest season to help pack the produce into punnets ready for transport to the railway station… I recall that Bourne watercress was transported to all the major markets throughout England, including Covent Garden.

One of the most colourful plants along our waterways is also one of the earliest to bloom: the marsh-marigold, which in mild years can be in full flower by early March. This species is deeply embedded in country folklore, as the host of traditional names attached to it testify. These include such charming titles as 'mollyblobs', 'horse-blob' and 'water bubbles', although 'king-cup' is perhaps the best known. Although still widespread and relatively common, this species has suffered, along with many others, as a result of drainage and bank 'improvement',

BOURNE WATERCRESS PLANTATIONS.
Prices on application to the
Proprietor E. N. MOODY.

Old water-cress beds can be a useful habitat for bird species such as green sandpiper and water pipit, as well as for mammals such as water shrew (see p.105).

ABOVE The colourful spikes of purple loosestrife have made this species a popular garden plant.

ABOVE RIGHT The marsh marigold is one of the most striking waterside species. 'Marigold' refers to the plant's historical association with the Virgin Mary.

species has suffered, along with many others, as a result of drainage and bank 'improvement', in which the marginal conditions it prefers are destroyed. These include water-meadows, now a decidedly rare habitat in Britain. Yet only 50 years ago waterlogged meadows, frothing in spring with cow parsley and other wild flowers, were a common sight alongside most natural waterways. These meadows were an integral part of the agricultural scene in the sense that they provided a rich source of spring and summer grazing for cattle and other livestock. Water-meadows were an ingenious system of landscape management, with the floodwater not only irrigating the pasture with natural nutrients, but also preventing the soil from freezing in winter. This meant that the grass would grow earlier in the season, thus enabling early lambs to make market by Easter. So the river helped the shepherd. There was a distinct art to this system, with the water-meadows requiring careful regulation, like a system of miniature canals. Their regrettable disappearance has been matched by the equally unwelcome demise of many associated plants and birds such as lapwing, redshank, snipe and yellow wagtail.

RIGHT The characteristic wing markings of the banded demoiselle make it one of the easier species of damselfly to recognise.

FAR RIGHT A common waterside inhabitant, the adult caddisfly resembles a moth in appearance. Its larvae are aquatic, and make protective body cases from pieces of river debris (see bottom of picture).

Peak flowering season for most waterside plants is May to July, when the bank can boast a riot of colour. One of only two native irises in Britain, yellow flag is a characteristic sight, alongside other species such as purple loosestrife, ragged robin, water mint, water forget-me-not and the delightfully named fine-leaved water-dropwort. These native plants are often joined by interlopers from overseas, introduced by plant-collectors into gardens, and which, having leapt the fence, are now happily naturalised across the country. Their presence is not always welcome, either; the invasive nature of both Japanese knotweed and Himalayan balsam is well known (both are now common waterside plants in parts of Britain), and the effect of Canadian pondweed can be even more serious, blocking sluices and drains and choking out more sensitive plants.

Jewels in the air

The light and shade of river life is complex, diverse and endlessly fascinating. This is never more apparent than in the rich summer extravaganza of colourful, cosmopolitan insects living above, below and on the water's surface. The delicate shimmering of dragonflies and damselflies is one of the main delights. Hovering effortlessly, they can disappear in an instant, off in pursuit of prey. The two can easily be told apart when at rest: dragonflies hold their wings flat and at right angles to their body, whereas damselflies fold their wings perpendicular to their abdomen. The life cycles of both start with the eggs being dropped onto the water or attached to the stems of plants. These then hatch into nymphs, which live underwater and are voraciously carnivorous and prepared to eat other pond animals, including tadpoles and small fish. It may take a full year before a nymph is ready to emerge from the water and undergo its metamorphosis into adult damsel- or dragonfly. Once in the air it will only live for a few dazzling weeks. Just under 50 species of dragonfly and damselfly have been recorded in Britain, and all are found near water. Several species are in decline, however, victims of habitat destruction and pollution, their nymphs poisoned by the run-off of agricultural chemicals into waterways. At one site in the Norfolk Broads the number of species dropped from 16 to just one over a period of 30 years, though such a dramatic decline is the exception rather than the rule.

Much decreased, the native white-clawed crayfish has disappeared entirely from some British river systems.

Fish and crustacea

One of the most beguiling and enigmatic river inhabitants is the white-clawed crayfish, a freshwater relative of the lobster and once a regular part of the diet of river folk. Measuring about 10 centimetres (2.5 inches) in length, crayfish live on the bottom of streams and small rivers, where they forage for vegetable and animal material among the pebbles and litter on the bed. They are both nocturnal and cannibalistic, often turning on their recently moulted brethren, who without their durable shells are temptingly tender. Sadly, white-clawed crayfish have declined massively in recent years as a result of habitat destruction, siltation, pollution (again the result of nutrient run-off from farmland) and 'crayfish plague', a fungal disease brought to British river systems by the introduced American signal crayfish, an escapee from crayfish farms. The plague is usually fatal to the native species, which is a Biodiversity Action Plan priority species and so subject to special protective measures. Although still widely distributed across Britain, populations of white-clawed crayfish are now thinly scattered and prone to sudden collapse. For example, the previously healthy population on the National Trust's Malham Tarn estate in Yorkshire appears to have become extinct recently – research is being carried out into the causes. Meanwhile, good numbers are present in parts of eastern Wales, the Peak District/Derbyshire (especially in Dovedale), northern England and the western counties of Northern Ireland. The species prefers alkaline water with limited sediment, low pollution levels and adequate shelter in the form of stones, aquatic plants and tree roots. Twenty-four per cent of the world's population is thought to live in Britain.

Two of the most remarkable fishy inhabitants of our waterways share equally dramatic life cycles. With both the eel and the salmon there is a sense of mystery and wonder attached to their extraordinary migrations, yet the distances and timings of their movements are diametrically opposed, and they have quite different life cycles and feeding patterns.

Eels spawn in the Sargasso Sea, north-east of the Caribbean. Their eggs are laid at great depths, then float to the surface, where they hatch. For three years, the larvae feed as they are carried across the Atlantic on the currents that feed the Gulf Stream. By the time they reach British waters, they are elvers: thin, translucent creatures sometimes called 'glass' eels. These feed on small snails and insect larvae, and seek freshwater rivers, wriggling inland on the full moon and high tide. They stay in rivers sometimes as long as 20 years, before feeling the urge to return to the sea. For this they choose a dark, autumn night with storms and no moon: the so-called 'silver eel' run. They migrate en masse, slithering across grassy fields to get back to salt water and open sea. They then make their way back to the Sargasso, where they spawn and the process starts again.

Eels, both young and old, were traditionally a popular food source and were often jellied. Some of the best eel smokers were the émigré Russian Jews in the East End of London, who started arriving in the late nineteenth century and used small brick kilns fired by oak chips to produce smoke. There are many ways of catching eels, Izaak Walton devotes no less than eleven pages to the eel in his *The Compleat Angler* (1653). One technique is 'clotting', whereby the worm is thread by a needle, using wool as the thread. About twenty threaded worms are then bound up into a single 'clot', and dangled into the water on the end of a stout stick. The eel grabs the worms in its mouth and its teeth become embedded in the wool. The skilled fisherman then yanks the eel out and drops it into a tin bath suspended over the surface of the water. This technique is still used today and is remarkably successful. The record stands at 80 eels caught in an hour. Other methods include using wicker baskets, metal grids set alongside weirs, or fyke nets – hooped nets which are laid on the riverbed, with an inner funnel. Once the eels swim in, they are unable to get out.

An equally popular river food in the past was lamprey, a freshwater eel lookalike with a characteristic circular disc on its face (actually a type of anchor used by the fish to move around over rocks on the riverbed, or to attach itself to other fish upon which it is parasitic). Lampreys were regularly eaten in medieval times and were often on the menu at banquets. A cookery book compiled *c.*1390 by the master-cooks to King Richard II contains a recipe for 'laumpreys in galyntyne', and a fifteenth-century recipe for lamprey in blood sauce exhorts the cook to

> Take a quyk lamprey…and sette the vessell with the blode vnder the lamprey while he rosteth;…And kepe the licoure that droppeth oute of him;…And cast a litull vinegre and parcely there-to, and a litul peper; And then take the blode and the dropping of the lamprey, and cast thereto pouder ginger, vynegre, salt, and a litull saffron; And whan the lamprey is rosted ynowe, ley him in a faire chargeour, And caste all the sauce apon him, And so serue him forth.

An adult pike is at the top of the waterway food chain, its speed and size a match for most other species.

The commonest of the three British species is the brook lamprey, although it has much declined in recent years, mainly due to river pollution. The strongest British populations today are found in Cumbria, south Wales and along the River Avon in Dorset, Hampshire and Wiltshire.

Whilst eels migrate from their birthplace towards the British Isles, the Atlantic salmon, Britain's only native species of salmon, chooses to come here to breed. Salmon spend several years at sea, feeding voraciously, before returning in spring to the rivers of their birth. To a salmon, each river has its own smell and signature, which it detects instinctively. After moving up the estuary, the salmon embark on a famous and remarkable journey upstream, vaulting over formidable obstacles until they finally reach shallow streams up in the hills, where they spawn. The spent adult salmon then drift back downstream. If they survive – by no means a certainty after all that exertion – they may migrate again the following year.

Despite this critical association with freshwater rivers, salmon are essentially saltwater fish. Indeed, the adults do not feed whilst they are in fresh water, and the vast majority of Britain's catch of salmon takes place in salt or brackish water, in estuaries and the lower reaches of rivers. However, there is a long tradition of catching salmon on rivers well inland, particularly in the north and west of Britain. One ancient method of taking salmon in Wales, once common on the Rivers Teifi, Severn and Wye, involved a short net slung between two coracles (see p.61). With great skill, two men would row silently downstream, trapping the salmon and taking them out of the net as they went. In other localities salmon were traditionally caught in conical traps. Called 'putchers' or 'kipes' and usually made of hazel or willow, these traps could be up to 5 or 6 feet in length. They were anchored to stakes and directed with the open neck facing upstream; the narrower waist at the other end was fitted to a smaller trap into which the fish would swim and not be able to turn round.

Traps were sometimes set in lines or stacked three-high in bolts. They are still used today on the River Parrett at Pawlett in Somerset and on the Severn near Lydney, for example. Salmon occupy a special place in river folklore, a legacy that extends to the present day via the enormous number of waterside pubs carrying names such as 'The Leaping Salmon'. There has, however, been a major decline in salmon numbers over recent years due to overfishing, and fishing licences have been withdrawn where possible. On some rivers sea trout are making a comeback.

The cultural associations that surround the salmon also extend to its smaller brethren, the trout. Brown trout are native to Britain, and are widely distributed in streams, rivers and lakes across the country. They are hugely variable in size, although most carry the characteristic red spotting on the flanks. They thrive particularly well in clear water, the crystal chalk streams of southern England providing particularly suitable habitat. Although trout form one of the main targets of the fly fisherman, they can also be caught by that ancient but well-attested technique, 'trout-tickling'. The secret is to quietly approach the bank and locate a trout that is lying close to the water's edge; then slowly put your hand into the water, very gently moving closer towards the fish until you are able to stroke its underside. So intoxicated is the trout by this sensation that it is possible to seize it and lift it out of the water.

By contrast, tickling is no way to catch a pike! Our largest freshwater fish, with records of specimens up to a metre and a half in length, the pike prefers to lurk out of sight, favouring rivers with plenty of bankside cover of aquatic vegetation. Arguably one of the most beautiful fish, it is a voracious predator, a quality that has brought into conflict with fly fishermen: trout are among the pike's preferred prey.

Mammals on the water

Living in, on or near water requires adaptation, and special characteristics are readily apparent in the mammal species that live along British waterways. These species range from the otter to the diminutive water shrew, and include both a recent and unwelcome interloper – the mink – and a characterful but sadly declined rodent, the water vole. One illegal immigrant, the coypu, was eradicated in the 1980s.

The otter is one of our most immediately recognisable mammals. The largest member of the weasel family, it is perfectly evolved for watery living: thick, water-resistant fur, webbed feet, small ears and a powerful tail that serves as a rudder. Otters are in essence solitary creatures (although cubs will stay with their mother for almost all of their first year) and feed primarily on fish, especially eels, although they will also eat small mammals, birds and amphibians. Until the mid-twentieth century the otter was widely distributed across the British Isles, and present in a range of waterside habitats, from upland streams to estuaries and rocky shore coasts. In medieval times otters were prized for their pelts, and were also regarded as having magical properties. The iconography of the animal was such that it appears in many place names: Ottery St Mary and the River Otter (Devon), Otterbourne (Hants), Otterhampton (Somerset) and Ottershaw (Surrey), for example.

In some areas otters were regarded as something of a pest, and during the nineteenth century otter-hunting became popular, complete with packs of otter hounds. In its heyday in the 1920s there were 23 such packs in Britain. At the National Trust's Llanerchaeron Estate in south Wales, one of the last of the Welsh gentry and hunting estates, otter-hunting was very much part of everyday life. The Llanerchaeron pack was made up of fifteen pairs of mixed English and Welsh foxhounds, with harriers, that hunted otter in the summer and fox in the winter. The huntsmen, with their blue coats,

After decades of decline, otter numbers are now increasing again and they are reappearing in many of their old haunts.

breeches and stockings, red cap, and waistcoat and tie, hunted far and wide from Swansea right up to Aberystwyth and had the run of nearly all the rivers of south Wales. Local fishermen, who were mainly after the sea trout, did not mind as the hunting stirred the river up. Otter-hunting ceased at Llanerchaeron in 1971 and the practice was finally made illegal nationwide in 1980.

By the 1960s a combination of hunting pressure, pollution and habitat destruction had led to a collapse in otter numbers. An animal that had once been a familiar sight to country folk had become nationally scarce and in some counties driven to extinction. Only in the last few years has there been something of a recovery in numbers (see p.133).

Although otter sightings are definitely on the increase, inexperienced observers can confuse the otter with another similar-looking species. The American mink is non-native, but in recent decades has successfully naturalised here, the population based on escapees from fur farms, particularly during the 1950s. Its arrival in the British countryside coincided with the demise of the otter, and the mink took full advantage of this event, moving with alarming rapidity across the countryside. Although it is much more catholic in its choice of habitat than the otter, it shows a definite preference for waterside habitats, where it hunts a wide range of prey, notably small rodents, birds and amphibians. The mink is an unforgiving hunter, killing virtually anything it comes across.

Growing mink populations have had a serious impact on ground-nesting bird populations in some areas, although there are signs that resurgent otter numbers may help stem the tide of mink; the otter is dominant, and will generally not tolerate mink in

Otter-hunting was once a popular country sport, yet was less responsible for the otter's twentieth-century decline than pollution and habitat loss.

its territory. Ironically, the abolition of otter-hunting coincided with the formal recognition of mink-hunting in 1978, although the latter practice is discouraged by most conservation groups due to the disturbance it causes to riverside habitats and to wildlife, including otters and water voles. The latter species has suffered considerable population declines in recent years, with mink being held primarily responsible. Although mink certainly predate water voles, habitat destruction and mismanagement are also likely to have played a major role in the demise of the vole.

One other mammal closely associated with water seems an unlikely candidate for riverside life. Daubenton's bat is most readily seen at dusk, swooping down low over rivers and lakes in pursuit of moths and other insects, which it will often pluck from the surface of the water.

Waterbirds

Wetland habitats are among the richest of all for birdlife, supporting a vast range of species. Some of these are resident birds, present in more or less the same habitat all year round, whereas others are summer migrants, taking advantage of the huge insect populations that gather in and near water during warmer conditions. Equally, autumn and winter bring migrants from the north, attracted by the rich feeding grounds that river valleys in particular can provide, especially when in flood.

The engaging water shrew is relatively common but rarely seen well. An excellent diver, it feeds on invertebrates and crustaceans.

Different types of waterway attract different types of bird. Rocky, upland streams are home to the dipper, an oversized member of the wren family, known mostly for its obvious white 'bib' and characteristic bobbing motion when perched on rocks mid-stream. The dipper feeds by plunging headfirst into the raging torrent. Then it walks along the riverbed or over underwater rocks, searching for invertebrates. Dippers are resident birds, although in harsh winter conditions they often move to lower altitudes where food is easier to find. Another denizen of hill streams is the grey wagtail, rather misnamed in the sense that the prevailing colour of the male in particular is actually the bright sulphur yellow of his underparts. Grey wagtails are not restricted to the uplands, however. In recent years they have become more widespread and common in lowland southern England, for example, and are often found in the vicinity of locks and weirs. Pied wagtails are common waterside birds, too, although less directly tied to water than their grey relatives. The migratory (and increasingly scarce) yellow wagtail is more a bird of water meadows and unimproved farmland.

Rocky hill streams are also a likely location in which to find one of our most delightful waders: the common sandpiper. Arriving in April from its wintering quarters in Africa, the sandpiper will take up territory along stretches of fast-flowing river, and lay its eggs in a shallow nest of grass tucked away between boulders near the water's edge. The fluffy chicks can feed themselves almost immediately after hatching, and come autumn will join their parents on the long journey south. Not all visitors to these northern rivers come from the south. In recent decades two species of essentially Scandinavian duck have increased dramatically and spread south, colonising many rivers in northern and western Britain. Both the goosander and red-breasted merganser belong to the sawbill group of ducks, so-called because of the serrated edges of their bills. Their preferred habitat is rivers with heavily wooded banks; the merganser nests on the ground among rocks or tree roots, whereas the goosander lays its eggs in tree cavities. Both species foresake their breeding grounds in winter, in favour of the coast (merganser) and large lakes or reservoirs (goosander).

ABOVE The sedge warbler can be distinguished from its close relative the reed warbler (*see* p.95) by its characteristic pale eye-stripe and striated back.

RIGHT One of only two native species of iris in Britain, yellow flag is a characteristic waterside plant. A coot passes by.

Few waterside birds are more well known or popular than the kingfisher. Decidedly exotic in its coloration, the kingfisher often appears as nothing more than a flash of electric blue and a piercing whistle as it flies away. Seeing one well requires patience and/or luck, yet this is a relatively common and widespread bird. Kingfishers can be found along almost any type of waterway, including coastal areas in winter, but during the breeding season, lowland rivers with exposed banks are particularly popular, as breeding takes place in tunnels excavated in the bank. Kingfishers are vulnerable to harsh winter weather, although they can recover their numbers well, laying six or seven eggs in each brood and with most pairs bringing off two broods in good years.

The dense stands of vegetation that are the hallmark of healthy waterways in spring and summer harbour a host of smaller birds. These include reed and sedge warblers, their harsh grunting and churring notes a characteristic sound of summer, as well as reed buntings and the enigmatic grasshopper warbler, usually detected by its monotonous song, unerringly like a fisherman's reel. The open water is, by contrast, the preferred domain of larger species of bird: moorhens and coots, grebes (both great-crested and little are common across Britain) and the mute swan, that most majestic of waterbirds, made famous by the ceremony of 'swan-upping' on the River Thames, when well-dressed men in livery scull up and down the river claiming swans, and weighing, measuring and ringing them. Finally, spare a thought for that long-legged dandy, the grey heron, a familiar sight to fisherman, towpath walkers and those travelling by boat, and described in my poem *Heron Fishing*:

Grey herons are common throughout much of Britain, and frequent a range of waterside habitats from estuaries to urban canals.

Sly sentinel	monocled hunchback
Vain admirer of his own reflection	lurks like sculpture
About to move	fleet and stabbing
The sharp punishing blade	darts
Fractures the water	pinions its prey
Swift purpose	gulps and gulps again.
Grey merging with sky	swallows silver on the green bank

Chapter Seven

❖

Reflections of grandeur

CASTLES AND MOATS

The association of water and architecture goes back to man's earliest times, to when the first rudimentary human settlements were established along the banks of rivers and edges of lakes. Access to water and to river transport, as well as defence considerations, all contributed to the proliferation of towns and villages along Britain's waterways. Control over the riverbank became a highly sought prize, and possession a source of prestige and power. Waterways became channels of control, and the buildings that lined them were increasingly perceived as symbols of authority. This arrangement – and the iconography it represented – was later adopted for use in the domestic context, with the advent of gardens and landscapes based around the artful and contrived deployment of water and other features.

The Normans were great castle-builders. At the time of Domesday (1087) 86 castles were recorded in England, a consequence of the Norman desire to dominate and subjugate. At first the Normans constructed traditional timber motte-and-bailey castles, complete with dry encircling ditches, but these later evolved into larger edifices of stone construction.

Paradoxically, the chief weakness of castles was their size. Although they might have appeared impregnable to attack, they could always be starved out or mined. However, as castles became bigger and more ambitious in design, a second weakness emerged: the higher the castle walls, the less easy it became for those defending from within, or from the ramparts, to exert control over what was happening down below. The foundations

Baddesley Clinton in Warwickshire, painted in 1898 by Rebecca Dulcibella Orpen.

Majestic Bodiam Castle
reflected in the waters of
its moat.

of such castles consequently became vulnerable to enemy attack. Using their shields as
protection, the enemy were able to excavate tunnels under the walls; they would then
insert wooden props to hold everything in place until they had adequately undermined
the castle structure. Next they would torch the props, which would collapse and bring
down the castle walls. The success of this approach led to a rethink in strategy on the
part of those responsible for castle design. Their solution was to use water as an ally in
their defence, through the construction of moats.

The earliest moats were created by damming valleys or by choosing to build on islands
or higher land, around which low-lying terrain, already prone to flooding, could be
excavated further. Moat-building really started in the mid-twelfth century and continued
in earnest till about 1320, although it was revived in the late Middle Ages, and then again
in Elizabethan times. Although moats originally had a military purpose, their construction
in later periods, after the invention of gunpowder, seems to have had far more to do
with status, prestige and paranoia than defence.

One of the most notable moated castles is that at Bodiam in Sussex, now cared for by
the National Trust. The castle was built in 1383 by Sir Edward Dalyngrigge, whose manor
house was located near the navigable river Rother, overlooking the Sussex marshes.
With the loss of English control over the Channel, Sir Edward felt his property to be
vulnerable to French attack. He therefore applied for a license from King Richard II for
the fortification of his manor on the condition that he protected the surrounding
countryside from French raiding parties.

The south façade of timber-framed Ightham Mote in Kent, seen through a hole in the moat wall.

The licence was granted, and the result is one of the most picturesque buildings in Britain. With a fine lake, three bridges, two islands and superb ramparts, Bodiam Castle was effectively a fortified island, offering all the modern conveniences of a fourteenth-century manor house: generous living accommodation (complete with fireplaces) and storage space, a well, pigeon loft, buttery, great hall, water gate, gatehouse and chapel. Although the interior is now in ruins, the castle appears surprisingly complete from the outside and its reflection in the water-filled moat is justifiably renowned.

With all castles, first impressions counted for everything. A moat set off a castle to best advantage, and gave it both scale and dignity. The reflection of the building in the surrounding water worked visually to double its size and impact. However, not all castles were moated. Many were built along rivers – serious castle construction took place at strategic river sites such as Windsor, Chepstow, Conwy, Ludlow, Newark and Warwick. Some of these castles were located prominently on bends in their respective rivers, and so needed no moat to enhance their defence. Most were owned and maintained by the Crown, and a combination of water and stone was used repeatedly to emphasise royal prestige and maintain central control over important riverine thoroughfares. Not to mention over the people that used them.

The usefulness of the moat to defend royal property and send psychological signals to one's opponents was not lost on the gentry. Moats were statements of grandeur, success and social status – the burgeoning baronial class found the temptation to emulate royalty irresistible. During the fourteenth and early fifteenth centuries a spate of moated manor houses appeared across England, built by wealthy barons and aristocrats who wished to enhance their prestige and authority. Of the 5,000 or so moats in England today, the majority are associated with manor houses dating from this period. The National Trust cares for some of the finest examples, including Ightham Mote near Sevenoaks in Kent, which dates from 1340 and nestles in a sunken valley. Interestingly, the word 'mote' actually comes from 'moot' meaning meeting place, but the half-timbered house is encircled by a delightful moat crossed by a small humpbacked bridge. In 1521, Sir Richard Clement bought the property for a bargain £400, and proceeded to modernise it with intriguing Tudor ornamentation and carving.

By this time wealthy landowners were able to concern themselves more with household comfort and architectural pretension than defence; many houses were expanded accordingly, but retained their moats as visual enhancements and statements of prestige.

Moats continued to have practical uses as a source of food. Often stocked with carp, pike and eels, they were also home to wildfowl, other foodstuffs such as watercress, and practical plants such as common reed, used in thatching. Yet it was their aesthetic contribution to the setting of the house in the landscape that became increasingly paramount. In some instances, such as at Scotney Castle in Kent (NT), the moat was later used as a focal point in the re-landscaping of the whole site. Here, the

Looking across the moat at Scotney to the Old Castle. The moat is the central feature around which the whole landscape works.

fourteenth-century moat is a central visual element in the garden created from 1837 onwards by Edward Hussey, the owner, and William Sawrey Gilpin, a leading exponent of the 'picturesque' style of garden design.

In addition to their undoubted aesthetic appeal, moats have a practical character that continues to strike a chord. At Helmingham Hall, near Stowmarket in Suffolk, the drawbridges over the moat are still raised every night, as they have been for almost four hundred years. We are, after all, an island race and to be an island within an island is the key to the moat's success. An Englishman's home remains his castle, although these days the drawbridge is more likely to be remote-controlled. Interestingly, new moats are still being constructed. The MI6 building, built in London alongside the Thames at Vauxhall in 1995 actually has two – just to be sure…

Riverside palaces

Castles were not the only large buildings built beside water. When James I came to the throne in 1603, there were no less than eight waterside royal palaces in England: Windsor, Hampton Court, Oatlands, Richmond, Westminster, Whitehall, the Tower of London and Greenwich. All of them were located in or near to London, and all were on the river Thames. The main reason for this was their accessibility. At a time when road conditions were generally poor, and even the most popular routes frequently impassable in winter or during bad weather, access by river was both reliable and more secure. Monarchs and their entourages passed from one palace to another in elaborate barges and boats.

The Palace of Westminster, originally built by William Rufus in 1097 on a site used by Canute, served as the principal residence of the kings of England from the middle of the eleventh century until the reign of King Henry VIII, who inherited the throne in 1509. Henry had been born in Greenwich and later favoured Greenwich Palace above all his other residences, expanding and embellishing it at great expense. The overall objective was for the palace to look at its most opulent and impressive from the river, by which means the most important visitors would arrive. Indeed, in 1527, Henry received an embassy there from the French king, François I. Henry's interest in Greenwich Palace was continued by his daughter, Elizabeth, who as queen used it as her main residence and made several additions to the building. Interestingly, the grounds of the palace are alleged to be where Sir Walter Raleigh famously threw his cloak over a puddle so his sovereign would not get her feet wet.

Engraving by James Basire (1730–1802) of the Palace of Placentia, or Greenwich Palace, from the River Thames. The building was demolished in 1694, for the building of Greenwich Hospital.

The old palace was considerably dilapidated by the time of the royal restoration in 1660, having served as a biscuit factory for part of the Commonwealth era. It was then demolished and replaced by a superb new palace based on designs by Inigo Jones. However, King William and Queen Mary, who ascended the throne in 1685, preferred to live at Hampton Court Palace, and so Greenwich Palace – one of the finest of its type in Europe – was incorporated into a naval hospital, although it continued to have strong royal associations.

To the west of London, Hampton Court Palace was the other great riverside palace. Thomas Wolsey, Archbishop of York and chief minister to Henry VIII, acquired it on a 99-year lease in 1515. He invested in it hugely, as a place in which to advertise his influential position and entertain his king, but Henry enjoyed it so much that he felt compelled to 'acquire' it from Wolsey. He then spent more than £62,000 (some £18 million in today's money) rebuilding and expanding it; he redesigned his own suite of rooms at least six times during his reign. Despite such investment, Hampton Court was only Henry's fourth favourite palace. He spent an average of 21 days a year there, far less than he spent at Greenwich.

Religion on the water

The Crown and the Church were the two most powerful institutions in medieval England and it is no surprise that the Church strove to match the monarchy, both in terms of its buildings and its infrastructural 'hardware'. Many cathedrals, abbeys and priories were built beside rivers, revealing a strange mixture of religious zeal and judicious control of water resources. Rivers brought in dues and levies on river trade, locks and fish weirs, as well as rent from mills, hostels and grazing rights over water-meadows. Yet at the heart of it all was prestige. The Church sought to exert as pervasive a degree of influence as the monarchy, and so chose the location for its own buildings carefully. Monasteries had long been located in remote situations, close to rivers and other water sources, but abbeys and bishops' palaces needed to be close to centres of population, so they could serve – and keep an eye on – the local community. Prestigious locations were chosen, so the appearance and stature of the building and its occupants were enhanced accordingly.

Often the construction of an abbey was the catalyst for the development of a town around it, however. Such is the history of Westminster in London, as described by Walter Harrison in 1776 in *A New and Universal History, Description and Survey of London and Westminster, Southwark etc*:

In antient times this was a mean unhealthy place remarkable for nothing but the abbey which was situated on a marshy island, surrounded on one side by the Thames and on the other by what was called Long Ditch. This ditch was a branch of the river which began near the east end of the place where Manchester-court is now built and ran by several windings to a little west of the gatehouse in Tothill St from whence it continued its course along the South wall of the abbey-garden, over which for many years past has been erected a common sewer. This island was an entire waste exclusive of the minster and was so overgrown with thorns and briers that from thence it was called Thorney Island. In process of time however a few houses were erected round the monastery which at length grew into a small town called West Minster.

One of the most impressive riverside religious palaces was that constructed on the river Trent at Newark in Nottinghamshire. Newark Castle was originally built by the Normans, but was remodelled at huge expense in the early twelfth century by

A hand-coloured steel
engraving of the partly
demolished Newark Castle,
c.1836, showing the
Romanesque gatehouse.

Alexander 'the Magnificent', Bishop of Lincoln and Lord of the Manor of Newark. The
result was a vast and impressive complex, designed to reflect Alexander's power and
prestige. Sadly, only twenty per cent of the building now remains; it passed to the Crown
during the Reformation and was later partly demolished on Parliamentary orders after a
siege in 1642. Thankfully, Alexander's superb three-storey Romanesque gatehouse
survives, as do stretches of the fourteenth-century walls. The castle's location, right on
the banks of the river, remains magnificent.

Water in the garden

Most early gardens in Britain had been associated with monasteries but the dissolution of
the latter in 1539, together with an increasing sense of peace and security in the country
at large, led to growing interest in the creation of what might be termed 'domestic'
landscapes. With defence no longer an overriding concern, landowners were able to
expand beyond the confines of their houses and look towards the creation of outside
spaces, in which they could relax and entertain. Utilitarian moats and fishponds were
adapted for more aesthetic purposes, with gardens increasingly conceived as settings for
grand houses, and as venues for elaborate display. This change coincided with the arrival in
England of new ideas from overseas, both in terms of garden design and content.

By the early seventeenth century, figures such as John Tradescant, gardener to Robert
Cecil and later to King Charles I, had visited not only the Low Countries but countries
as diverse as Russia and Algeria. Gardeners became explorers and plant-collectors, and
merchants brought back stories of exotic creations like the Moorish Alhambra in
Granada, with its water gardens and fountains. They also travelled to Constantinople,
Persia and India, where gardens often incorporated running water to bring down cool
mountain air and so alleviate the stifling heat. These ideas were distilled for use in English

conditions, and spawned a series of innovative new gardens featuring the use of water. One of the most important of these was at Hatfield in Hertfordshire, where Tradescant laid out a splendid new garden and Salomon de Caus designed an elaborate system of waterworks. De Caus was the author of *Les raisons des forces mouvantes* (1615), a book dedicated to the explanation of hydraulics and an essential reference source for all those keen to introduce complicated water features in their gardens. It was no longer enough to have water present in the garden as an inert feature; it had to be active, energetic and alive, a goal achieved via the use of fountains and cascades. 'Water jokes' became popular, whereby jets of water would shoot out over unsuspecting passers-by.

One early and delightful first-hand account of the playful role of water in gardens is by Celia Fiennes, and appears in her celebrated travel diary. In 1685 she visited Wilton House, where extravagant formal gardens had been laid out by Isaac de Caus (brother of Salomon) c.1630. These included some jovial Italianate water features and a particularly entertaining grotto:

> In the middle of the roome is a round table, a large pipe in the midst, on which they put a crown, or gun or a branch, and so it spouts the water through the carvings and points all round the roome at the Artists pleasure to wet the Company; there are figures at each corner of the roome that can weep water on the beholders and, by a straight pipe on the table they force up the water into the hollow carving of the roof like a crown or coronet to appearance, but is hollow within to retaine the water forced into it in great quantetyes, that disperses in the hollow cavity over the room and descends in a shower of raine all about the roome.

View of the statue of Neptune in the centre of the arm of the T-Canal at Westbury Court Garden, Gloucestershire. The mid-seventeenth-century statue was reputedly found in the River Severn in the early eighteenth century.

In 1688, William and Mary of Orange took the throne. Garden design changed yet again, with Dutch formality and knowledge of water management adding a new dimension. In Holland, canal-building was a highly sophisticated affair, and water was used to great effect, both in the landscape and, increasingly, the garden. The best surviving example in Britain of a formal water garden in the Dutch style can be found at Westbury Court in Gloucestershire, now owned by the National Trust. Dating from 1696–1705, the garden was constructed out of low-lying water meadows alongside the river Severn. Its centrepiece is a 450-foot-long canal, with a fountain at one end and a two-storey pavilion at the other. The emphasis is very much on symmetry, order and control, with the water marshalled to formal effect.

As the eighteenth century progressed, ideas on how water should be used in the garden changed in favour of a more relaxed, naturalistic effect. Water would harmonise with the natural landscape, rather than the former dominating the latter. This change can be seen at the very fine water garden created by John Aislabie and his son, William, at Studley Royal in North Yorkshire (NT), between 1716 and 1781. Aislabie Senior had been Chancellor of the Exchequer but was expelled from Parliament over the South Sea Bubble fiasco. All his energies then went into the extraordinary garden he created in the valley of the river Skell, with the ruined Fountains Abbey as its focal point. Today the simplicity of the original concept shines through. The river Skell, after passing Fountains Abbey, is drawn down beyond

ABOVE **Henry Hoare II's epic landscaped garden at Stourhead, showing the Palladian Bridge and the Pantheon.**

RIGHT **The naturalistic landscape of Studley Royal Water Garden created by John and William Aislabie.**

a bend, before being turned and led down, more formally this time, via a cascade into a shallow canal, where it passes classical temples mirrored in the circular and semi-circular ponds. The river then flows over another cascade into a large lake. Here, again, are pavilions, temples and towers strategically dotted around the woods and gardens. The feeling is quite magical, and representative of the then contemporary fashion for juxtaposing water with architecture.

A similarly epic landscape was created at Stourhead in Wiltshire (NT), again using water as a vital component. Created by Henry Hoare II between 1740 and 1785, the landscaped valley garden took its cue from Hoare's experiences on his 'Grand Tour' and from the paintings of Claude, Poussin and Gaspar Dughet. Here, art was mirrored by landscape design and the gardens were, in turn, mirrored by the lake. The 'picturesque' was born, and the natural resources of the young river Stour were used to the full. From Six Wells Bottom and St Peter's Pump the river is led to the River God and the Nymph of the Grot. Originally there were fishponds and two smaller lakes, but these were combined to make one large lake in the 1740s. Thousands of trees were planted, bridges and temples were commissioned, all focused on the watery paradise created at the heart of the garden.

Men such as the Aislabies and Hoare made classical and European ideas of perfection their own, blending them into the English landscape and using water as an integral component. Landscape became viewed as an art form, a subtle and ingenious beauty that would mature long after its creators were gone. Such figures were not just experimenting with the English landscape, they were inventing it. The feeling they worked to create, of relaxed spontaneity and of nature half-tamed, gave the world something quite remarkable. A few lines from Alexander Pope, from his 1731 *Epistle IV* to Richard Earl of Burlington, exemplifies the philosophy behind contemporary trends in English landscape design:

Weeping willows were introduced from the Far East in the eighteenth century and soon became popular in landscape parks on account of their elegant form and foliage.

119

To build to plant, whatever you intend,
To rear the column or the arch to bend
To swell the terrace or to sink the grot
In all let nature never be forgot
But treat the goddess like a modest fair
Nor over dress or leave her wholly bare
Let not each beauty everywhere be spied
Where half the skill is decently to hide
He gains all points who pleasingly confounds
Surprises, varies and conceals the bounds.

Consult the genius of place in all
That tells the water or to rise or fall.

The area of Biddulph Grange known as 'China', looking south from the 'Temple' across peaceful waters to the footbridge and Joss House.

All the leading landscape gardeners of the day used water, but none more so than Lancelot 'Capability' Brown, the leading exponent of landscape 'improvements' in the 1750s and 1760s. Water played an ever more important role in his world, becoming very much the key to his landscapes. He ambitiously dammed or re-routed rivers, creating new lakes or expanding existing ponds into vast swathes of water designed to set off the house and landscape park to maximum effect. One of Brown's most successful commissions was at Petworth in Sussex (NT), where in 1752 he created one of the supreme achievements of eighteenth-century landscape gardening in Europe. Brown's forte was the creation of serpentine lakes, formed by damming small streams and using the subtle curves and contours of natural valleys to produce the desired effect. Waterfalls, cascades, islands and swans were *de rigueur*, as were optical illusions and perspective. There was also much artistic licence, extending to the creation of 'deceivers' such as false bridges. Everything was designed for effect.

Brown's projects were invariably epic, but smaller-scale works could be just as successful and pleasing. This was particularly so in the nineteenth century, when the emphasis turned increasingly towards the exotic, if not downright fantastic. One of Britain's most extraordinary Victorian gardens uses water modestly, but with enormous impact. In the 1840s, James Bateman, his wife Maria and their friend Edward Cooke, a marine painter, made an extraordinary series of gardens at Biddulph Grange in Staffordshire (NT). Biddulph is effectively a miniature tour of the world, ranging from Egypt, complete with a pyramid, to a delightful stream-fed glen masquerading as a Himalayan valley (once full of rhododendrons, now replaced by ferns). At the centre of the garden is 'China', based around a delightful 'willow pattern' design. It features a pond spanned by a Chinese bridge and with a brightly painted temple on its bank. Seahorses, gilded dragons, hanging bells and carved grebes complete the effect, the whole ensemble delightfully reflected in the water below.

Using water to create beauty in the landscape is an old trick, yet enduringly successful. The transition from defensive moat to gurgling rill is complete, a trite end perhaps to a significant journey which en route has produced one of the greatest British contributions to art: the landscape garden, complete with skillfully designed lake, cascades and fountains. Perhaps it is no coincidence that mini-canals now feature regularly at the Chelsea Flower Show, and that Princess Diana's memorial in Hyde Park will be a water feature. The success of water in the landscape is such that television garden makeovers are now able to concoct a mini-Stourhead out of even the smallest back garden.

Chapter Eight

❖

Water futures

WATER OWNERSHIP AND WATER QUALITY

We've followed the journey of water from source to sea, seen how it has powered industry, given birth to waterside communities, provided a haven for threatened plant and wildlife, and played a key role in landscape design. The fate of our waterways is now in the balance. And the prospects are mixed. The increased concentration of water supplies in the hands of a small number of multinationals creates opportunities but also risks, and we continue to pollute our precious water resources while demanding the highest standards in terms of quality. The restoration of canals in particular has revitalised a number of inner-city communities, yet the upsurge in waterside leisure and recreation brings its own pressures.

On planet earth, 98 per cent of our water is salt water and only 2 per cent fresh water. Of that 2 per cent, most is locked up as ice – 87 per cent to be precise. This leaves 13 per cent available as fresh water, of which 12 per cent is groundwater and only 1 per cent free-flowing water in rivers and lakes. In other words, visible fresh water amounts to 0.02 per cent of all the water on the planet. Most scientists agree that global warming is starting to trigger climate change. This means that management of finite water resources will become an ever more important and contentious issue in the decades to come. Even in a rich, fertile European country such as ours, which has more than adequate rainfall, careful management of water is still a key factor to our survival.

The question of water ownership in Britain is a fascinating – and often surprising – one. Who actually owns the groundwater in the aquifers, the water in lakes and rivers, or the water that flows from the tap? All of us? None of us? The Environment Agency perhaps? Or the water companies?

In a sense, the question of who owns water is an academic one; it is the access to that water and the rights associated with it that count. Whoever has that access, and therefore those rights, has power, but with this power comes responsibility. Wading through water legislation is certainly a time-consuming business. A vast body of ancient law exists which reaches right back to Saxon times, giving individuals and institutions such as monasteries and priories rights to build bridges, locks, weirs and dams. Most legislation states that the water in between riverbanks in tidal estuaries is owned by the Crown, as is the foreshore up to the highwater mark. From source down to the estuary the banks and bed are technically owned by those who own the land on either side, ie the riparian owners. If two different riparian owners are involved, one on each side of the river, as is often the case, the mid-point of the river is taken as the fluid boundary. Yet these riparian owners do not own the water itself, only rights to its abstraction – usually 20 cubic metres a day for domestic or agricultural use (excluding spray irrigation). This equates to 20,000 gallons or the capacity of two milk tankers. Other uses require abstraction licenses. The raindrop one inch above the farmer's field (or your garden lawn) does not belong to anyone. At one time the Crown might have thought that it owned the water and the rivers, but in effect it did not. Parliament's claim is equally as tenuous.

PREVIOUS SPREAD Lord Foster's shining steel and aluminium Millennium Bridge has helped transform the capital's South Bank.

Water is a free agent, almost always on the move, and like the fish, it is wild. But having rights to fish those wild fish is quite another can of worms… Fishing rights are jealously guarded night and day by certain water bailiffs and gangs of watchers, particularly where salmon are concerned. The interests of fly fishermen are often set against the much more ancient hereditary rights of salmon netters and those using fixed engines. The rules of hereditary fishing state that a fisherman can only pass the right to fish onto his children or close relatives. In return, a licence fee must be paid and netting times are restricted and closely monitored. These often ancient rights do imply obligations both ways — they are a hangover from the feudal system, which not only limited the activities of the lower classes, but often did so in such a way as to conserve stocks. It is only modern methods that have taken such a large toll on the fish.

Today it is usually the Environment Agency that monitors and administers our water courses, with responsibility for flood defences and pollution monitoring, and with the power to grant abstraction licences to water users. The Environment Agency does not, of course, own the water it administers; the ownership of water rights is an assumed right but not an absolute one, an anachronism which has existed since time began. We rely on the water companies to give us a constant supply of clean drinkable water, and to treat our dirty water with care and then send it on downstream, for the next abstraction and purification cycle. And we rely on watchdogs like Ofwat, the Drinking

Salmon netting on the Tamar in Cornwall, opposite Cotehele Quay.

Water Inspectorate and local authority environmental health teams to keep the water companies in order. This may sound reasonably straightforward, but with our regional water companies now in the hands of a small number of powerful private companies, with their inevitable duties to offshore shareholders and directors, achieving balanced control is no easy feat.

Water has not always been concentrated in the hands of so few. The Victorian era saw a boom in water companies, which were invariably inaugurated by Acts of Parliament and regulated by general legislation and local authority rulings. Water was often filtered through sand, but bacteriological examinations were not routine until 1885. Chlorine was first added to drinking water at the time of the First World War. The Second World War no doubt concentrated people's minds wonderfully when it came to strategic resources and with the 1945 Water Act began a national overview of the various water companies… and there were a lot of them. In 1946 there were 1,226 but by 1970 the number had fallen to 198. The Water Act of 1973 created the ten large water companies we know today, based, wherever possible, on clearly defined catchment areas and river systems, and this in effect marked the beginning of a national policy for water. The rest of the country is catered for by smaller companies, although some, such as Essex and Suffolk Water, still supply around 1.7 million households. On 1 September 1989, the ten water companies were privatised and ownership is now concentrated in the hands of a small number of multinationals, the largest players being two French conglomerates. Yet there has been successful resistance. In response to a hostile takeover bid of Hyder (Welsh Water) from US Western Power Distribution in 2001, Hyder set up an innovative 'not for profit' water company. Similarly, the Cholderton and District Water Company Ltd, one of the last of the small locally distinctive water companies, still supplies 2,100 consumers in three villages near Salisbury with water, and the National Trust also supplies many of its own farms and cottages.

The Craig Goch dam in the Elan Valley, south Wales. The Elan Valley reservoirs, constructed in the 1890s, were designed to supply the city of Birmingham with much-needed water.

Of course amidst the vagaries of legislation one thing we know for sure is that water itself is far more powerful than any court of law, Parliament or water company. In times of flood we are all too keen to disown water, to open the sluices and send it on downstream. In times of drought we suddenly stop washing our car and golf courses have their sprinklers sabotaged. The conglomerates would like you to think that they own your water, but they are only intermediaries, and have transitory rights. True, we as consumers ought to be consulted more often, but we also have a responsibility to take an interest in where our water actually comes from and who controls it. The constant stream of new converts to domestic water filters does at least show that we do care about water quality, and that we are prepared to pay for it. And the popularity of ancient water rites such as well-dressing ceremonies is evidence that we are keen to reconnect at source with water in a collective sense too. Perhaps in twenty years' time the National Health Service will be using hydrotherapy along with rag wells, mud baths and water meditation.

Recent flooding of the River Severn at Upton-upon-Severn, Worcestershire. With annual mean temperatures rising, inhabitants of many UK towns will do well to prepare themselves for more of the same.

Après le déluge

Excessive rainfall and floods, monsoon conditions, violent storms, strange temperature changes, droughts... you name it, we've had it. The facts are that in this country mean temperatures have risen 0.7°C (1.26°F) since 1659, when temperature records began, and most of this has been since the year 1900. Global temperatures are predicted to rise by between 1.4 and 5°C (4.5 and 9°F) by the year 2100. The 1990s were the warmest decade for a thousand years.

Scientific opinion generally concurs that this rise in temperature is due to human activity of one sort or another. The rise is also too high to be part of natural fluctuations. The results will be modified rainfall patterns and a tendency towards more extreme weather. In crude terms this means that prolonged flooding and flash flooding are more likely. This is exactly what we have seen in this country with the increasingly dramatic summer floods over recent years, such as the one that occurred on the Somerset Levels and Moors in August 1997, and which caused extensive damage to wildlife as the floods swamped the low-lying fields of hay, wheat and maize. The crops rotted, the water heated up very quickly, many fish were killed by the anaerobic conditions and the food supply was threatened. Swifter drainage from agricultural land and vast acres of new concrete and tarmac mean that rivers rise much faster than they did 50 years ago and these problems, combined with a rise in sea levels, mean increased flood risks – and they do not bode well for insurance premiums. Some coastal villages may even have to be abandoned.

If we are to deal successfully with the problems of flooding then the reinstatement and protection of our wetland areas is essential (see p.134). There are great hopes in this context for a piece of EU legislation known as the Water Framework Directive, voted in by the European Parliament in 2000 (http://europa.eu.int/comm/environment/water/water-framework/index_en.html). Its title may be uninspiring, but this is a far-reaching and comprehensive ruling that has been heralded as a major environmental landmark. As well as reinstatement of wetlands, the Directive also instructs member countries to force households into using water in more efficient manner (through metering, among other things).

Since the end of the Second World War, we have lost 94 per cent of our bogs, three-quarters of our reed beds and two-thirds of our grazing marsh. At one time a quarter of Britain consisted of wetland. At many wetland reserves, the pumps in summer now work not to drain the land but to keep the water level up, to provide habitats damp enough for waders and other species. In Northern Ireland alone, two-thirds of the redshanks and lapwings have gone, along with half of the curlews and a third of the snipe since 1986 – a tragic loss. All this in aid of a state-subsidised agriculture that has been overproducing for two decades. What's more we choose, stupidly, to build on our flood plains, and the run-off from roofs and gutters, concrete aprons, tarmac, roads, business parks and housing developments is now so immense that the natural water courses cannot cope.

The hope is that, wherever possible, wetlands will re-emerge and provide, as they always have done, a refuge for excess water and thus enable the associated wildlife to thrive once more. It's as well to take a glance back in time also, to what nineteenth-century writers had to say about the wetlands. John Clare, in *To the Snipe*, wrote of the undrained fens:

> *Here tempests howl Around each flaggy plot,*
> *Where they who dread man's sight the waterfowl*
> *Hide and are frightened not*

Charles Kingsley took a more pragmatic view, once the fens had been drained:

> *Gone are the ruffs and reeves, spoonbills and avocets…*
> *ah well at least we shall have meat, mutton instead and no more*
> *typhus and ague.*

While Gerard Manley Hopkins had a poetic, laissez-faire approach in *Inversnaid* (1881):

> *What would the world be, once bereft*
> *Of wet and wildness? Let them be left,*
> *O let them be left, the wildness and wet,*
> *Long live the weeks and the wildness yet.*

Water innovations – art & architecture

Water has always been an inspiration to artists of every shade and hue. Alongside the struggle to protect our precious wetland wildlife, and to curb floods and pollution, has emerged in recent years a whole range of innovative new waterfront buildings and structures, and groundbreaking arts and music projects.

The new generation of elegant footbridges, which like exotic dragonflies hover delicately over beautiful stretches of water, have been a much-talked about addition to Britain's architecture. The real delight of these footbridges is that they are silent, not thundering with traffic noise. You can sense the fluidity, the tide and the power of the river. The Norman Foster-designed 'Blade of Light' bridge, with its low-slung steel cables, stainless steel balustrades and aluminium decking, which crosses the Thames and connects Tate Modern with the City (bridging the gap between Art and Finance), was certainly the forerunner in terms of media coverage, but turned out to be a victim of its own success. The Great British Public, longing for a new experience – 100,000 of them to be precise – walked over the bridge on the first weekend. The enthusiastic marchers found to their dismay that the bridge wobbled alarmingly. Months of research resulted in a new system of dampers, which seems to be working, though it will no doubt be even longer before the structure loses its moniker of 'the wobbly bridge'. Also in the capital, the new Hungerford Footbridge, a cable-stay footbridge with decks suspended from inclined steel pylons, hangs on either side of the Charing Cross rail bridge. The crossing dates from 1845, when Isambard Kingdom Brunel designed a suspension bridge to serve Hungerford Market at Charing Cross. Brunel's original chains were later shipped down to Bristol where they were resurrected as the Clifton Suspension Bridge.

The Hungerford footbridge,
connecting Waterloo Pier to
the Embankment, is a beautiful
night-time spectacle.

Twenty-seven new bridges were in fact funded by the Millennium Commission. The new 'winking eye' bridge on Tyneside, designed by Wilkinson Eyre and connecting Newcastle with Gateshead by the Baltic Flour Mills Art Centre, is surely one of the most ingenious. The single-span structure is shaped like an eyebrow or a lyre waiting to be plucked, and is a fine addition to other famous Tyne bridges such as Robert Stephenson's 1849 High Level bridge, William Armstrong's 1,450-ton central Swing Bridge, built in 1876, and Mott Hay and Anderson's New Tyne Bridge, opened in 1928 and a prototype for the Sydney harbour bridge.

Another single-span arch is the new Lowry Footbridge at Salford Quay, the inland port at the end of the Manchester Ship Canal. The bridge is raised on steel ropes at a height of 60 metres (197 feet) and opens vertically from both sides to let ships through. It has transformed the post-industrial landscape of Salford and, with the Lowry Arts Centre nearby, has helped bring about a real regeneration of the area.

In a more rural setting, the Shanks Bridge near Peterborough connects the Fen with the town, forming a major link in the Green Wheel network of cycleways, bridlepaths and footpaths. The Nene is navigable down to Wisbech via the Dog and Doublet lock and up to Northampton, where there is a connection with the Grand Union Canal. The Torrs Millennium Walkway in Derbyshire, meanwhile, threads its way through a gorge cut by the River Goyt. At one point it is cantilevered over the river in a curve from a railway retaining wall and then supported by a series of T-shaped pillars. Like the Lowry it is a triumph of local initiatives over industrial dereliction.

Bridges are not the only new structures to catch the eye on our waterways. A particularly arresting sight is *Willow Man*, a sculpture by Serena de la Hey arising from the Somerset Levels and reflected in the moat below. Standing at over 12 metres

Willow man by Serena de la Hey. The sculpture has a skin of interweaving willow, sourced from the heart of the Somerset Levels, and an internal steel framework.

(40 feet), *Willow Man* is caught in mid-flight running alongside the M5 near Bridgwater. Tragically, someone set light to the sculpture in early May 2001. The public outcry was huge. Serena was interviewed on Radio 4, explaining what she would like to do to the man responsible (we assume it was a man), and local steel erectors, radio stations, farmers and willow growers all helped with the rebuild. The moat that now surrounds the sculpture was in part a reaction to this vandalism. Over 60,000 vehicles a day pass the sculpture, which means that with an average occupancy of 1.5 per vehicle over 90,000 people a day view *Willow Man* from the M5 alone.

In an age of increasing awareness about local distinctiveness, the work of Common Ground stands out. Along with organising Apple Days, saving orchards, inspiring parish maps and a whole host of other music and arts projects, Common Ground created the Confluence music project, based on the River Stour in Dorset. Karen Wimhurst, composer-in-residence for three years, and music animateur Helen Porter composed more than 220 new pieces of music for the project. There were 50 performances and hundreds of workshops. New choirs and even orchestras were formed, including a plumbing ensemble called Pipeworks playing, amongst other things, the Bog Horn, the Immersion Beater, the Down Pipes and the Ballcock Maracas. Members of the Bournemouth Sinfonietta also played at several concerts. The starting point was the National Trust's Stourhead, and the Stour and its many tributaries were at the heart of the project. Birdsong was woven into chamber ensembles, environmental issues were aired, oral history plugged, Tibetan bowls with water inside played. Slowly the project worked its way downstream past Wincanton, Gillingham, Sturminster Newton, Blandford and Wimborne. The last concert was held in Christchurch Priory near the harbour where the Wiltshire Avon and the Dorset Stour meet. The finale was a large-scale choral work called Silver Messenger, composed by Karen Wimhurst and with my own libretto. It involved over 120 singers, 25 musicians, and soprano Frances Lynch. Confluence was an ambitious music and water project and yet one which could be repeated on any river system in the world.

New environmental initiatives

There are so many new wetland and river conservation schemes afoot in Britain that it is impossible to highlight more than a handful. Boosting salmon numbers, encouraging otter populations, and reinstating fenland, rank among the most important.

Looking across the pond near the Hide at Wicken Fen, a haven for invertebrates and other precious fenland wildlife.

Salmon fisheries are always an emotive subject and the encouragement of salmon numbers is the focus of considerable effort in many parts of the country. One project is to construct seventeen new fish passes on the River Kennet, putting back in place those weirs that were on the river in the eighteenth century. As the Kennet connects with the Thames, this will enable Thames salmon to reach the higher streams to breed. Salmon numbers are also being helped by the buying out of net fisheries. In many parts of the country net limitation orders are now in place, with the aim of eventually reducing the number of nets to zero. Thirty years ago, 45 per cent of salmon returning to spawn were grilse (young salmon on their first return from salt water). Today this is 75 per cent – an encouraging sign which will considerably aid stocks.

The otter is another conservation success story. Recent survey work has revealed that there has been a fivefold increase in otter numbers since the first national otter survey was carried out in 1977–79. At that time otter populations in most parts of Britain were perilously low, and the species was totally extinct on several major river systems. During 2000–02 signs of otters were found at 34 per cent of the wetland and river sites surveyed, up 22 per cent in just ten years. Much of the increase is due to cleaner water and more sympathetic riverside management, as well as strict legal protection. As recently as 1977 otters were still being hunted with hounds. Threats remain, however. City-centre waterside developments, so beloved of planners and local authorities, can be bad news for resurgent otter populations, which are trying to recolonise urban sites. Far too many otters are killed on roads, too. This usually happens when rivers are in flood under bridges, forcing the otters up to road level. The Wildlife Trusts have been working with the Highways Agency to identify localities where this is a particular risk, with the aim of installing 'otter underpasses' to help reduce the death toll.

With three hundred years of sustained drainage and agricultural improvement, the decline in the wetland areas of East Anglia has been marked. One interesting scheme which has been given the go-ahead is the reinstatement of reed beds on the Great Ouse at Holywell-cum-Needingworth near St Ives in Cambridgeshire. Around 445 hectares (1,100 acres) of arable farmland will be returned to reed bed after gravel extraction. The site, administered by the RSPB, will create the largest area of reed bed in the country and will help boost the numbers of bitterns, as well as waterfowl, marsh harriers, otters, water voles and possibly even spoonbills. As recently as 1997, the bittern was virtually extinct. Since then the population of the well-camouflaged bird has nearly quadrupled, thanks to intensive work to recreate the homes that had been lost to drainage and destruction. The scheme requires some complex engineering. The water level has to be kept below the surrounding level, so clay linings must be put in place to keep the gravel pits from forming one massive lake. Bitterns are also high on the agenda around Lakenheath, where the restoration of reed beds is greatly helping their numbers – a strange reversion to nature after all the efforts of Cornelius Vermuyden and his drainage gangs in the seventeenth century.

Similarly, at the National Trust's Wicken Fen, plans are afoot to acquire an additional 3,700 hectares (9,143 acres) of farmland to the south and so enable the continuing sustainability of the area. The Fen was first established as a nature reserve because of its invertebrate populations, of which nearly 7,000 species have been identified, including more than 120 that feature in the Red Data Book of rare invertebrates. Extending the boundaries will help reduce the risk of extinction for individual species and make possible migration between populations. In addition, it is hoped that peat, the Fenland's most precious resource, will begin to grow again after three centuries of decline. Also at Wicken Fen, König ponies are being used to keep the vegetation down and so maintaining the wet conditions needed for Fenland wildlife to thrive.

New canal projects
Britain's canals, so often the victims of neglect, have been enjoying a true renaissance in recent times. Canals are being restored and reopened at the same rate of knots as they were being built during the era of canal mania in the 1790s. The scale of regeneration is enormous, much of it helped by Lottery funding and regiments of volunteers, and this second coming of canals is a fitting tribute to their original engineers.

The Rochdale Canal was the first-ever trans-Pennine canal. After 50 years of inactivity, 32 miles of canal, from Sowerby Bridge near Halifax to Manchester, have now been restored. Known as the 'Everest' canal – it rises 183 metres (600 feet) over the Pennines – it has 91 locks and forms a direct link between major industrial and urban centres. The canal looks certain to bring benefits to the inner-city areas along its course. The town centre of Failsworth near Oldham, for example, is undergoing a complete transformation, with new canalside business and leisure developments. Ancoats in East Manchester, an area much in need of regeneration, is reaping similar rewards. Overall the project has created around 820 new homes and 4,000 jobs. Wildlife also benefits considerably. A particularly precious feature of the Rochdale Canal is its population of water plantain (see p.89). Scientists worked carefully to preserve the species during construction, relocating them to reserve sites before any work began and using an underwater digital video camera to record vital information.

Another trans-Pennine canal is the Huddersfield Narrow, originally built between 1794 and 1811. It runs for 20 miles and its restoration involves the reopening of the Standedge Tunnel near Marsden, which at 3¼ miles long, 194 metres (638 feet) below ground and 2.1 metres (7 feet) wide is the longest, deepest and highest canal tunnel in the UK. The canal then descends from Diggle to Ashton under Lyne, where access is gained to the Cheshire Ring via the Ashton Canal. To even contemplate taking a canal over the Pennines in the first place required great nerve, yet there are three canals that do so, the third being the Leeds and Liverpool. These ingenious canals are an extraordinary and beautiful feature of the northern landscape.

In the south, the Kennet and Avon is another example of a long-term restoration project now nearing completion. Here, 87 miles of a canal closed since the 1950s have

Part of the Manchester city-centre section of the Rochdale Canal, where it plunges into a dark underworld below the modern buildings of Piccadilly. Piccadilly Lock can be seen between the pillars.

been reopened, though work remains to be done to stabilise banks and locks. The Kennet & Avon contains some of the country's most impressive water architecture, including the imposing Avoncliff Aqueduct near Bradford-on-Avon. Conservation of these historic structures was a major part of the restoration. At Bradford-on-Avon itself, two new 100-berth marinas have helped local business and this, together with towpath improvements, have made the waterside a booming leisure area. Establishment of a reed bed at Sells Green has helped local populations of frogs, kingfishers and dragonflies but the species most aided by the restoration is the endangered water vole, the focus of a number of environmental schemes.

Waterside recreation

Canal restoration obviously offers considerable opportunities for leisure activities and enterprise, though not all schemes meet with universal approval. The possible reopening of the Suffolk Stour, with 13 locks from Sudbury to the sea, has been violently opposed by, among others, the descendants of John Constable the landscape painter. The Constable family claims that the introduction of mass leisure boating would destroy the quiet, winding river landscape that the painter immortalised. They have a point, but commercial horse-drawn barge traffic was operating there until 1935. The effect of recreational activity on waterways is something that is being closely monitored in the Norfolk Broads. The Broads form a unique waterway landscape: 125 miles of lock-free, navigable waters. The task for the Broads Authority, who administers the area, is to balance the demands of one million annual visitors with the environmental needs of the area. With a range of leisure uses including sailing, motor-boating, rowing, canoeing, fishing, walking and birdwatching, there are inevitably conflicting pressures. One way to limit environmental damage is to encourage the use of electrically powered boats as opposed to motorised craft, which cause riverbank erosion and loss of reedswamp (as well as being major noise polluters). Speed limits also help reduce the level of bank erosion. Zoning, whereby some types of craft are excluded from the most sensitive areas, helps solve conflict between users, and limiting the numbers of new moorings is an obvious way of reducing the number of craft on the Broads. Even boat design is being looked at. Research has shown that long, fine bows reduce wave-making, so reducing erosion, and the Broads Authority works with boat manufacturers to incorporate such aspects into hull design.

The government also appears to be taking waterways seriously and has published its first policy document on the subject for 30 years. A large-scale return to water transport is unlikely but not impossible. Currently three million tons of material (primarily rubbish, coal and building materials) are carried on water, mostly in the North East, and this figure could double in ten years. In the future, canals might even be used as a means of moving large quantities of water around the country from the North West to the South East. An intriguing prospect.

It is, of course, difficult to please everyone. Water does and always will arouse deep passions. But to understand water, you really do have to get your feet wet. You have to swim. You have to feel it surround you. You have to experience the rivers in all seasons, to admire their reflections and their angry moments. They are the repositories of countless generations, let it not be said that we ignored them. In the words of Roger Deakin, that great adventurous Suffolk swimmer of stories and writer of rivers and moats: 'Water is the most poetical of elements, allowing of no sudden awkward movements, even a stone dropped in sinks gracefully.'

Kingfishers have long been associated with folklore. In Elizabethan times, a dead kingfisher, suspended by a thread in the air, was believed to always turn towards the direction of the wind, and kingfisher feathers were valued as a talisman against lightning.

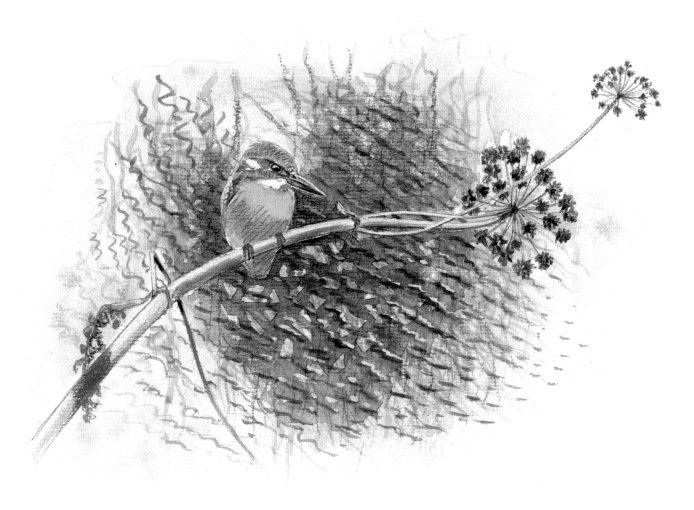

Places to visit

The National Trust cares for almost 250,000 hectares (617,750 acres) of the most beautiful countryside in England, Wales and Northern Ireland. Waterways owned and looked after by the Trust include watermills, moated castles and manor houses, canals and moorings, wetland areas, rivers and streams, all of which offer outstanding opportunities for recreation and nature-watching.

The places to visit that follow are just a selection; fuller information on many more National Trust places of landscape and wildlife interest is available in the Trust's Coast and Countryside Handbook or from the network of Trust regional offices, details of which can be obtained from the following address:

The National Trust Membership Department, PO Box 39, Warrington, WA5 7WD, tel. 0870 458 4000, fax 0870 609 0345, **enquiries@thenationaltrust.org.uk**

A view from the lake at Stourhead, one of the National Trust's many fine landscaped gardens, where water and nature work in harmony.

County	West Glamorgan
Property	Aberdulais Falls

The River Dulais flows through a deep wooded gorge, rich in wildlife, before cascading over sheer sandstone cliffs. For over four hundred years these famous waterfalls provided the energy to power the wheels of industry, from the smelting of copper in the late sixteenth century through corn-milling and iron-working to a tinplate works that finally closed in the 1880s. This dramatic and beautiful site was frequented by famous artists, including Turner in 1796, and it remains a popular visitor attraction today. The river has been harnessed once more to produce electricity, with a modern turbine contributing to the national grid and an 8-metre (27-foot) waterwheel enabling the property to be self-sufficient in environmentally friendly power. The turbine house provides access to an interactive computer, fish pass, display panels and observation window. There are magnificent views, both from here and from the top of the falls proper.

The river contains sea trout and salmon, and is especially notable for its waterbirds, such as dipper, grey wagtail and kingfisher. There have also been sightings of otter, both on the river and beneath the waterfall. Interesting species of fern and moss can be found in the wooded gorge.

Access
Three miles north east of Neath, signposted from the A4109 and four miles from the M4 (exit 43 at Llandarcy, follow the A465 signposted 'Vale of Neath'). The visitor facilities are open seasonally (charge for non-National Trust members) and events are held throughout the year. Further information is available on 01639 636674.

When to visit
The falls are at their most dramatic following heavy rain, whilst the wooded gorge is particularly beautiful in autumn, when the leaf colours can be magnificent.

County	Antrim
Property	Patterson's Spade Mill

A relic of Ireland's agricultural past, Patterson's is the last surviving water-driven spade mill in the country. Founded in 1919 and run as a family business for over 70 years, the mill was used to produce a variety of implements ranging from light tools for flower beds to heavy-duty spades for cutting turf. The mill fittings are intact and well preserved, and spades are now being made again. Two hundred or so are produced each year, and are available for sale at the property.

The mill is particularly suitable for educational groups, and there are hands-on activities to help explain the fascinating and highly skilled processes involved in tool-making.

Access
The mill is located two miles north-east of Templepatrick on the A6 Antrim–Belfast road; take exit 4 of the M2. Open between March and September, but days and times vary, so visitors are advised to check in advance on 028 9443 3619. There is an admission charge for non-National Trust members.

When to visit
A range of special events is held at the mill throughout the open season, varying from a craft and country fair to themed days such as 'Farming in the '40s'. Further details are available from the property.

County	Derbyshire/Staffordshire
Property	Dovedale

One of the most celebrated landscapes in the Peak District, Dovedale is part of the National Trust's South Peak Estate. The River Dove winds its way through a magnificent gorge, with the steep-sided slopes cloaked in ash trees and topped by limestone outcrops and pinnacles. The word 'Dove' comes from the Saxon word *dubo*, meaning black, a reference to the dark appearance of the water in parts of the river, caused by the bed being heavily vegetated.

The area's superb scenery has made it a popular visitor destination for centuries, with the Victorians laying the famous 'Stepping Stones' that lead across the river. Wildlife abounds, with birdlife especially notable. There are nesting jackdaws and redstarts in the caves and rock cavities, dippers and kingfishers along the river, and ravens and buzzards overhead. Goosanders occur throughout the year. The cave systems are home to bats, and the scree slopes above the river support interesting communities of mosses, lichens and liverworts.

Access
Dovedale lies west of the A515, north of Ashbourne, and is open all year. The main access points are at the southern end of the dale, off the minor road between Ilam and Thorpe, and from the northern end via Milldale. There are car parks at both ends (not National Trust), and an unmanned information point at Milldale. Refreshments are available at Polly's Cottage (seasonal, non-National Trust). A footpath leads through the dale. Further information is available on 01335 350503. There is also a National Trust shop and visitor centre at Ilam Park, near the southern entrance to the dale.

When to visit
Although sometimes bleak, winter at Dovedale can be delightful. There are fewer visitors than at peak times in the summer and the structure of the limestone landscape is at its dramatic best when the trees are bare of leaves.

County	Surrey
Property	The River Wey and Godalming Navigations and Dapdune Wharf

The Wey, one of the first navigable British rivers, opened to barge traffic in 1653. Extending some 15 miles, it linked Guildford to Weybridge on the Thames, and provided access to London. The Godalming Navigation, which opened in 1764, enabled barges to work a further four miles upriver. The award-winning National Trust visitor centre at Dapdune Wharf, Guildford, tells the story of the navigations and of the people who lived and worked on them.

The waterways act as an important ecological corridor. Cormorant and common tern are among the more interesting birds, and the wetland areas support populations of scarce plants such as marsh stitchwort, marsh cinquefoil and narrow-leaved water dropwort. Insects include the very rare white-legged damselfly.

Habitat management includes coping with a range of non-native and potentially invasive species. Signal crayfish (see p.100) have increased dramatically in recent years and Himalayan balsam is a problem along some banks. One of the most serious problems is created by floating pennywort, an arrival from North America during the 1980s. It creates dense mats over the water's surface, smothering native plants and de-oxygenating the water so fish and aquatic invertebrates cannot survive.

Access
Dapdune Wharf (open seasonally, charge to non-National Trust members) is on Wharf Road in Guildford, to the rear of Surrey County Cricket Ground off Woodbridge Road (A322). There is a car park, and easy access from the town centre and railway station on foot via the towpath. The boatyards where the huge Wey barges were built can be visited here, as can *Reliance*, one of the last surviving barges. Boat trips are available in season. A network of towpaths, extending some 20 miles in total, provides access along much of the navigations. Access to the navigations is also possible at Godalming Wharf (off the A3100) and at Pyrford, where parking is available at 'The Anchor' pub. Visiting craft can enter the navigations from the Thames at Shepperton or the slipways at Guildford, Stoke or Pyrford. Visitor moorings are available at Dapdune Wharf by arrangement and in many places along the towpath side of the navigations.

When to visit
High summer is the perfect time to explore the navigations. The banks are a riot of colour, with meadowsweet, purple loosestrife and watermint all in evidence.

County	Bath and North East Somerset
Property	Prior Park Landscape Garden

Set in a sweeping valley with magnificent views over Bath, Prior Park was created between 1734 and 1764 by local entrepreneur Ralph Allen, with advice from the poet Alexander Pope and celebrated landscape designer Lancelot 'Capability' Brown. Although one of England's most significant designed landscapes, this is a surprisingly intimate place, with many interesting features and carefully contrived vistas. The water running through the valley was dammed to create three small lakes and a series of cascades, over one of which spans the famous Palladian bridge, one of only three surviving in Britain. There is open access to most areas of the park. Despite its proximity to the city, the park is home to a wide variety of wildlife, with birds such as little grebe, heron and kingfisher, and good numbers of dragon- and damselfly. The lakes are stocked with carp, tench, perch and chub and, perhaps not surprisingly, there is also evidence of otter activity.

A five-minute walk from the garden leads to the Bath Skyline, an historical landscape of woodland and meadow also rich in wildlife.

Prior Park College, a coeducational school, operates from the mansion (not National Trust).

Access
The park is open throughout the year, but days and times vary, so visitors are requested to check in advance. There is an admission charge for non-National Trust members. All visitors must use public transport as there is no parking at Prior Park or nearby. Further details on access are available on 01225 833422.

When to visit
Spring is an especially delightful time at Prior Park, with swathes of wild garlic and the range of trees and shrubs looking particularly fine when coming into leaf.

| **County** | Cornwall |
| **Property** | Cotehele Quay |

One of several historic ports on the River Tamar, Cotehele Quay has been associated with Cotehele House, rebuilt mainly between 1485 and 1627, since medieval times. The house, with its dovecote, garden and orchard, nestles in a sheltered combe above the river. Cotehele Quay has historically been significant for the importation of stone, slate, coal and lime, which was later burnt in the limekilns alongside the quay. In the nineteenth century the Tamar valley was extensively mined for tin, copper, silver and arsenic. Much of the tin ore was sent downstream to be smelted at Cargreen, while copper ore went by sailing vessel to south Wales. Plums, apples, mazzard cherries, daffodils and early potatoes were also important in the Tamar valley and were sent downriver in Tamar barges to Plymouth.

Cotehele Quay is home to the restored Tamar sailing barge the *Shamrock*. There is a tea-room called the Edgcumbe Arms on the Quay and a small museum that tells the story of river trade. Up the Morden valley, a restored watermill produces stoneground flour. In summer, a ferry operates from Cotehele Quay upriver to Calstock.

Sea trout and salmon are common in the Tamar and occasionally can be seen jumping out of the water. Reedbeds on either side of the river are host to ducks, moorhens, reed warblers, sedge warblers, kingfishers and snipe. Herons are frequently seen and further down the Tamar at Weir quay avocets can often be spotted in autumn. Little egrets are now resident and otters are fairly common. At Cotehele Mill in late spring you can see the southern marsh orchid.

Access
Cotehele Quay can be reached by road and is accessible at all times. It is one and a half miles southwest of Calstock by steep footpath (six miles by road), eight miles southwest of Tavistock, and fourteen miles from Plymouth via Saltash Bridge. Calstock can be reached from Plymouth by water (contact Plymouth Boat Cruises Ltd, tel. 01752 822797) and from Calstock (tel. 01822 833331). Cotehele Mill is open seasonally, so visitors should check in advance on 01579 351346.

When to visit
One of the best times is early spring, when the many varieties of Cornish daffodil are out. In May look for apple and cherry blossom. Later in the summer enjoy the strawberry season and of course apples in the autumn. A Cornish Food fair is held at Cotehele in early November.

Further reading

The following is a list of useful books and articles for those who wish to find out more about waterways. Many can be found on the shelves of public libraries, through which the more obscure titles can often be ordered.

Chapter 1
Francis Bond, *Fonts and Font Covers*, OUP (1908)
Dorothy Hartley, *Water in England*, MacDonald (1964)
J. Meyrick, *A Pilgrim's Guide to the Holy Wells of Cornwall*, J. Meyrick (1982)
Alan Neal, *Dowsing in Devon & Cornwall*, Bossiney (2001)
M.L. Quiller-Couch, *Ancient and Holy Wells of Cornwall*, Chas. J. Clark (1894)
Peter Naylor and Lindsay Porter, *Well Dressing*, Landmark Publishing (2002)
Norman Wilson, *The Tap Dressers*, Country Books (2000)

Links to examples of dewponds, spas and wells:
www.dewponds.com
www.bathspa.co.uk
www.malvernspa.co.uk
www.chalicewell.org.uk

Chapter 2
Common Ground, *The River's Voice*, Green Books (2000)
Common Ground, *Rhynes, Rivers & Running Brooks*, Common Ground (2000)
James Crowden, *In Time of Flood*, Parrett Trail Partnership (1996)
www.commonground.org.uk
www.england-in-particular.info

Chapter 3
Dan Curtis, *Going with the Flow: Small Scale Water Power*, CAT (1999)
Derwent Valley Mills and their Communities, Derwent Valley Mills Partnership (2001)

Ray Holland, *Micro hydro electric power*, ITDG (1986)
Small Scale Hydro Schemes, ETSU (1996)
Leslie Syson, *British Watermills*, Batsford (1965)
Leslie Syson, *The Watermills of Britain*, David & Charles (1980)
R.H. Taylor, *Alternative Energy Sources*, Adam Hilger Ltd (1983)
John Vince, *Discovering Watermills*, Shire Publications Ltd (1970)
www.ukmills.com
www.microhydropower.net
For a list of funicular railways in the UK see
www.rinbad.demon.co.uk/gb_funi.htm and
Engineering Heritage Vols 1 & 2, Institute of Mechanical Engineers (1963 & 1966)

Chapter 4
John Adamson, *Along the Arun*, The Alexius Press (1994)
Paul Atterbury, *English Rivers & Canals*, Artus Books (1984)
William Camden, *Brittania* (Edmund Gibson's 1586 edition), Unicorn & Black Swan (1695)
Eilert Ekwall, *English River Names*, OUP (1928)
Celia Fiennes, *The Journeys 1685–1703* (Christopher Morris ed.), Cresset (1947)
Mark Girouard, *The English Town*, Yale University Press (1990)
Walter Harrison, *History, Description and Survey of London*, Shakespear's Head (1776)
Josephine Jeremiah, *The River Severn: A Pictorial History*, Phillimore & Co. (1998)
Richard and Nina Muir, *Rivers of Britain*, National Trust/Webb & Bower (1986)
John Rogers, *English Rivers*, Batsford (1948)
Nathaniel Spencer, *The Complete English Traveller*, Shakespear's Head (1772)

Chapter 5
Nick Billingham, *Waterways Images From An Industrial Age*, Tempus (1999)
Harold Bode, *James Brindley*, Shire Publications Ltd (1999)

Anthony Burton, *The Canal Builders*, M & M Baldwin (1993)

Anthony Burton and Derek Pratt, *Canal*, David & Charles (1976)

Anthony Burton and Derek Pratt, *Anatomy of Canals: The Early Years*, Tempus (2001)

Hugh Conway Jones, *The Gloucester and Sharpness Canal*, Tempus (1999)

H.C. Darby, *The Draining of the Fens*, CUP (1940)

Robert Davies, *Canals of the West Midlands*, Tempus (2001)

Clive and Helen Hackford, *The Kennet and Avon Canal*, Tempus (2001)

Avril Landsell, *Canal Arts & Crafts*, Shire Publications Ltd (1997)

Derek Pratt, *Discovering London's Canals*, Shire Publications Ltd (1977)

L.T.C. Rolt, *Narrow Boat*, Alan Sutton (1994)

L.T.C. Rolt, *Navigable Waterways*, Longmans (1969)

Peter Smith, *Canal Architecture*, Shire Publications Ltd (1997)

Peter Smith, *Canal Barges & Narrowboats*, Shire Publications Ltd (1994)

Peter Smith, *Discovering Canals in Britain*, Shire Publications Ltd (1997)

Mike Taylor, *The River Trent Navigation*, Tempus (2000)

Michael Ware, *Canals and Waterways*, Shire Publications Ltd (1995)

Michael Williams, *The Draining of the Somerset Levels*, CUP (1970)

www.britishwaterways.co.uk
www.thewaterwaystrust.com
www.englishwaterways.com
www.environment-agency.gov.uk/subjects/navigation

Chapter 6

Bruce Campbell and Donald Watson, *The Oxford Book of Birds*, OUP (1964)

W.H. Dowdeswell, *Ecology: Principles and Practice*, Heinemann (1984)

John Evelyn, *Sylva*, Royal Society (1664)

Richard and Alastair Fitter, *Wild Flowers of Britain*, Collins (1974)

Archie Miles, *Silva*, Ebury Press (1999)

Roger Phillips, *Trees in Britain*, Pan (1978)

Roger Phillips, *Grasses, Ferns, Mosses & Lichens of Great Britain and Ireland*, Pan (1980)

Izaak Walton, *The Compleat Angler* (Edward Jesse ed.), Bohn's Illustrated Library (1861)

Chapter 7

Hugh Braun, *The English Castle*, Batsford (1936)

Sylvia Crowe, *Garden Design*, Garden Art Press (1994)

Roger Deakin, 'Moats' in *Gardens Illustrated* (June 2001)

Laurence Fleming and Ian Gore, *The English Garden*, Michael Joseph (1979)

Marilyn Symmes (ed.), *Fountains: Splash and Spectacle*, Thames & Hudson (1998)

Christopher Thacker, *The History of Gardens*, Croom Helm (1979)

Kenneth Woodbridge, *The Stourhead Landscape*, The National Trust (1982)

Chapter 8

www.ofwat.gov.uk
www.water.org.uk
www.serenadelahey.com
www.dwi.gov.uk (Drinking Water Inspectorate)
www.dundee.ac.uk/law/iwrli (International Water Law Research Institute Dundee)
Countryside and Rights of Way Act (2000).
Available at:
www.hmso.gov.uk/acts/acts2000/20000037.htm
Second Consultation Paper on the Implementation of the EC Water Framework Directive (2000/60/EC) DEFRA. Available at:
www.defra.gov.uk/Environment/consult/waterframe2/pdf/waterframe2-2.pdf

National Trust Publications

The National Trust publishes a wide range of books that promote both its work and the great variety of properties in its care. In addition to more than 350 guidebooks on individual places to visit, there are currently over 70 other titles in print, covering subjects as diverse as gardening, costume, food history and the environment, as well as books for children. A selection can be ordered via our website **www.nationaltrust.org.uk** and all are available through good bookshops worldwide, as well as in National Trust shops and by mail order on 01394 389950. The Trust also has an academic publishing programme, through which books are published on more specialised subjects such as specific conservation projects and the Trust's renowned collections of art.

Details of all National Trust publications are listed in our books catalogue, available from The National Trust, 36 Queen Anne's Gate, London SW1H 9AS – please enclose a stamped, self-addressed envelope.

Waterways is the fourth in the National Trust series *Living Landscapes*. Appreciation of landscape dates back centuries, but a balanced understanding of the value of human interaction with the environment has only come about more recently. Through *Living Landscapes* we aim to explore this interaction, drawing on the vast range of habitats and landscapes in the Trust's care and on the bank of expertise the Trust has acquired in managing both these and the wildlife they support.

Each book in the series will explore the social and natural history of a different type of landscape or habitat. Beautifully illustrated with specially commissioned artwork and a range of stunning contemporary photographs and historical material, this series will appeal to all those with an interest in social history, wildlife and the environment. Further details are available on our website (see above).

Picture Credits

P1	NTPL/Joe Cornish	P69	Museum of London
P4	Jamie McCullough	P70	The Bridgeman Art Library
P9	James Crowden	P71	British Museum
P10	NTPL/Stephen Robson	P72	NTPL/John Darley
P12	NTPL/Erik Pelham	P74	Science & Society Picture Library
P13	Mary Evans Picture Library	P76	James Crowden
P14	Mary Evans Picture Library	P78	The Royal Geographical Society
P15	NT	P79	NTPL/John Darley
P16	Fiona Screen	P81	The Royal Geographical Society
P18	Tim Guthrie	P82	James Crowden
P19	Bill Glenn, Earthhart Photography	P83	British Waterways
P20	James Crowden	P84	NTPL/John Hammond
P22	Courtesy of Bath Archaeological Trust	P86	MEN Syndication
P23	Courtesy of Roman Baths Museum, B&NES Council, Bath	P87	Greater Manchester County Record Office
P24	View Pictures Ltd/Edmund Sumner	P88	James Crowden
P25	NTPL/Joe Cornish	P90	NTPL/Will Curwen
P26	NTPL/Joe Cornish	P97	Rex Needle
P28	NTPL	P104	James Crowden
P31	NTPL/William R. Davis	P108	NTPL/Andrew Butler
P32	NTPL/Derek Croucher	P110	NTPL/John Hammond
P34	NTPL/Derek Croucher	P111	NTPL/Andrew Butler
P36	NTPL/John Hammond	P112	NTPL/Ian Shaw
P37	Guildhall Art Gallery, Corporation of London	P113	NTPL/David Dixon
P38	Guildhall Library, Corporation of London	P114	Guildhall Library, Corporation of London
P40	Trevor Ermel	P116	Fiona Screen
P42	By permission of the National Library of Wales	P117	NTPL/Mike Williams
P44	Mary Evans Picture Library	P118	(top) NTPL/David Dixon; (bottom) NTPL/Andrew Butler
P45	The British Library	P120	NTPL/Nick Meers
P46	NTPL/Mike Williams	P122	Grant Smith/VIEW
P49	NTPL/Ray Hallett	P124	James Crowden
P50	Derby Museum and Art Gallery	P126	Welsh Water
P51	Derwent Valley Mills Partnership	P127	Richard Packwood/Oxford Scientific Films
P52	NTPL/Mike Williams	P129	Sally-Ann Norman/VIEW
P53	NTPL/Dennis Gilbert	P130	Tim James/VIEW
P54	NTPL/Andrew Butler	P131	Paul Tyagi/VIEW
P56	NTPL/Roger Hickman	P132	Bill de la Hey
P59	NTPL	P133	NTPL
P60	The Royal Geographical Society/John Speed	P135	www.penninewaterways.co.uk
P61	Museum of English Rural Life, The University of Reading	P139	NTPL/David W. Gibbons
P62	Chiswick Library Local Collection	P141	NTPL/Andrew Butler
P64	James Crowden	P143	NTPL/Dennis Gilbert
P65	NTPL/Lee Frost	P145	NTPL/John Darley
P66	The Royal Geographical Society/Z. Allnut	P147	NTPL/John Darley
P67	NTPL/Andrew Butler	P149	NTPL/David Noton
P68	Museum of London	P151	NTPL/Andrew Salter

Index

A

B

C